THE
QUALITY *of* MERCY

THE GENTLER VIRTUES
IN GREEK LITERATURE

BY

GRACE H. MACURDY

PROFESSOR EMERITUS OF GREEK
VASSAR COLLEGE

NEW HAVEN

YALE UNIVERSITY PRESS

LONDON · HUMPHREY MILFORD · OXFORD UNIVERSITY PRESS

1940

*The publication
of this book was in part made possible
by the
J. Leverett Moore Research Fund in Classics*

To

GILBERT MURRAY and J. A. K. THOMSON

Interpreters of Hellenic thought

PREFACE

IN writing this book, in which I consider the subject of humanity in Greek literature and the evidence which that literature offers to disprove the belief that the Greeks were "not humane by instinct" and that their feeling for mercy and pity was greatly inferior to that of modern men, I have drawn from many sources. The sources directly cited are mentioned in the footnotes. I owe especial acknowledgments and thanks to several scholars and writers who permit me to quote from their works, Gilbert Murray and C. M. Bowra of Oxford University, J. A. K. Thomson of King's College, London University, F. M. Cornford and F. L. Lucas of Cambridge University, W. W. Tarn and E. R. Bevan. I thank Dr. Mary Ely Lyman of Union Theological Seminary in New York and Professor Florence B. Lovell of Vassar College for kindly giving me information and references for the dating of various books of the Old Testament. Miss Fanny Borden, Librarian of Vassar College, has assisted me, as always, by procuring books from other libraries, and her staff has been most courteous and helpful to me during the many hours spent in the Library. I am grateful to my friends and colleagues in the departments of Greek and Latin in Vassar College for the interest which they have taken in my work.

I esteem it a high privilege that I am permitted to contribute a volume to the publications issued in celebration of the seventy-fifth anniversary of Vassar College and in honor of President Henry Noble MacCracken.

G. H. M.

Vassar College,
February 19, 1940.

CONTENTS

INTRODUCTION

THIS book discusses the growth of the humane virtues developed early by the Greeks and reflected in their literature to the end of Athenian independence. Beginning with the epic *aidos,* which signifies the sense of shame that keeps a man from a base act and often assumes the meaning of mercy and pity, I have considered the feeling for humanity and the gentler virtues which is expressed in Greek poetry, chiefly in epic and tragedy, and in the historians and Attic orators of the fifth and fourth centuries B.C. These virtues are finally comprehended in Justice, as it appears in the Platonic dialogues and in Aristotle, who calls Justice "the perfect virtue" and "virtue entire."

It was with reluctance and with fear that the Greeks learned the value of the higher meaning of *aidos,* of which the god Apollo says, "it proves a great hurt as well as a great help to men." The Homeric heroes feared it; Agamemnon bitterly reproached his brother for feeling it; and Achilles asked the spirit of his friend Patroclus to forgive him for yielding to it. The heroes had the primitive and savage dread of pity that Nietzsche expresses when he says: "Pity is opposed to the tonic emotions that heighten the energy of life-consciousness *(Lebensgefühl)."* Though his heroes have this fear of pity, the poet who turned the songs of bloody battles and cruel death into a moralized poem with tragic meaning knew the beauty of *aidos* and deepened the sense of pity in the word.

Hesiod extols *dike,* the right way, the righteous judgment, and hates cruelty and oppression. His conception of *dike* leads to *dikaiosyne,* abstract justice, which became the most important virtue of the aristocratic sixth century and one of the chief democratic virtues of Athens in the fifth century. Justice is celebrated with a steadily expanding and enriched meaning from Theognis in the sixth century, who is among the first to say that in it all virtue is embraced, to Plato who "desired to build a city wherein Righteousness dwelleth," like the new heaven and new earth of the writer of the second Petrine Epistle.[1]

The verses that Aristotle quotes from Euripides in praise of justice—"O golden face of Justice, nor morning star, nor evening star so marvelous as this"—reveal the lyric motion of the Greek in contemplating the perfection of moral excellence.

It is obvious that this conception of perfect justice, which, as Plato proves, does good to foe as well as to friend, is close to St. Paul's *agape,* which "taketh no account of evil." In St. Paul's strangely beautiful and thrilling outburst of praise of love, we see the culmination of all that the Greek spirit had experienced in morality from the time that it was first moved by the tender feeling of *aidos.*

The sober-minded Aristotle says in the *Ethics* something about friendship that might have been written by St. Paul about *agape,* his "charity" or "love,"—"where men are friends, there is no need of justice."[2]

In spite of the warnings that are often given that one must look to the more commonplace writers, such as Xenophon and the Attic orators, for the true ethical and humane feeling of the Greeks, I have thought it of higher value to consider more fully what the great epic and tragic poets say and what their beliefs were in questions of humanity and "virtue." It was they who exercised the profound and lasting influence over the thought of the Greeks, and they who passed on the precious inheritance to Plato and Aristotle and the Hellenistic writers, which finally reached the New Testament, and became part of our western ideals of mercy,

1. J. Adam, *Republic of Plato,* I, 242. Cambridge, 1926.
2. Aristotle, *Ethics,* 1155a, 4.

right, and justice. These ideals are now darkened by the influence of ignorance and cruelty, but we may still say of them what Antigone in face of death said of her Unwritten Laws: "Their life is not of today alone, nor yet of yesterday, but it goes on forever."

THE QUALITY OF MERCY

I

MERCY AND PITY, *AIDOS* AND *ELEOS*

WHEN Lecky[1] said that the plays of Euripides were the first revelation to the ancient world of the supreme beauty of the gentler virtues, he had in mind the virtues that spring from a sense of humanity; that is, pity,[2] mercy, regard for others, and loving-kindness, the opposite of cruelty, insolence, and selfishness. He calls the Altar of Pity in Athens the "first great assertion among mankind of the sanctity of mercy," and notes that the Greek spirit from a very early period was distinguished for its humanity.

It is true that these gentler virtues which appear in the literature of the Greeks have a unique flowering in their tragedy. The most striking and most hotly discussed statement in Aristotle's definition[3] of Greek tragedy is the final phrase in which he says that it is by pity and fear that tragedy affords an outlet for emotion. He finds an unhappy ending the most tragic, since it arouses the two emotions most poignantly, and, therefore, he holds that Euripides is the most tragic of the poets[4] because most of his plays end unhappily.

Of course, the tragic element in a play is not necessarily measured by its ending.[5] Such a play as the *Alcestis*, prosatyric and ending "happily," has many tragic scenes. Eurip-

---

1. W. E. H. Lecky, *History of European Morals*, I, 228 f. New York, 1929. Cf. F. L. Lucas, *Euripides*, p. 34; New York, 1928.

2. Aristotle, *Ethics*, 1105b; *eleos*, pity, classed among the emotions. The abstract *eleemosyne* is a later formation.

3. *Poetics*, 1449b. 4. *Ibid.*, 1453a.

5. H. Weinstock, *Sophokles*, p. 227. Leipzig and Berlin, 1931. "Nur eins zunächst ist nötig, aber auch unumgänglich, die Tragödie zu schaffen: Leid."

ides is the great master of tears and it is his constant appeal to the emotion of pity that lends support to Aristotle's statement. He is a conscious advocate of the human virtues, a hater of cruelty, and constantly makes propaganda in his plays against the oppressor, whether against a barbarous tyrant such as Lycus in the *Heracles Furens,* or a merciless state (Athens, by implication, in the *Trojan Women*). The beauty of self-sacrifice and mercy and the exceeding sinfulness of *hubris* (insolence) are painted by Euripides with such obvious and conscious intention that sometimes in his plays the artist is lost in the preacher. But the preaching is always on the side of the angels.

One of his most subtle and true utterances is the passage in the *Electra*[6] about the quality of mercy:

> There is no pity in the ignorant.
> The wise man pities and he pays the price
> In pain, for being wise and pitiful.

The insight of these words is Athenian and Euripidean. They belong to the time of Socrates and the sophists and are in spirit the counterpart of Socrates' famous paradox about the identity of goodness and knowledge.

Centuries before Euripides lived and wrote the gentler virtues appear in the oldest extant work of the Greek genius in poetry, composed in the early Iron Age. In spite of the fact that the *Iliad* is an epic of war with long descriptions of battles and bloodshed, which no doubt gave pleasure to the audiences which heard the epic recitations, the poem is infused with the pity that lies at the heart of tragedy. Aristotle saw this[7] and said that the *Iliad* is tragic, a poem of suffering, while the *Odyssey* is "ethical," a story of characters. Plato also calls Homer, meaning the author of the *Iliad,* the master of noble tragedy.[8] There is comedy in the *Iliad,* but

6. *Electra,* 294 ff. My translation.

7. *Poetics,* 1459b, 9, 14. Cf. W. Rhys Roberts, *Longinus* (Cambridge, 1899) p. 200, "*ethos* as contrasted with *pathos* was considered a special mark of comedy as distinguished from tragedy."

8. *Theaetetus,* 152 E, *Republic,* 595 C.

it is generally the gods who are made comic. Mortals are sorrowful and tragic.

Not all readers of the *Iliad* have discovered the tragic humanity of the poem. To William James,[9] for example, it seems, like history, "a bath of blood"—"one long recital of how Diomedes and Ajax, Sarpedon and Hector *killed*. No detail of the wounds they made is spared us, and the Greek mind fed upon the story." If the *Iliad* were only a long recital of bloody exploits of prehistoric heroes, in the manner of the suspected tenth book, it would not deserve to be called tragic and probably would have vanished like its predecessors. But some great genius (perhaps other lesser ones before him also) has humanized the old sagas by infusing them with gentler things, the love of friend for friend, of husband and wife, love for a child, and mercy shown to enemies.[10]

The *Iliad* is the story of the effects of *hubris,* wanton insolence, the Greek equivalent of sin;[11] of *aidos,* the equivalent of conscience in the early Iron Age, being the scruple that keeps a man from shameless and inhumane acts; and of *eleos,* mercy. The moral ideals of the Iron Age, in which the *Iliad* was composed, were in some respects less high than the most civilized codes of today, but there is no indecency in the *Iliad* and no condoning of cruelty. The poem is "a representation of serious subjects in a grand kind of verse."[12] It differs from tragedy not in spirit, but in presentation, being limited to one kind of verse and to the narrative form, and not limited in time to the "single circuit of the sun," within which the action of a Greek tragedy is, with few exceptions, contained.[13] The *Iliad* has the power of tragedy to

9. *Moral Equivalent for War,* p. 4. New York, 1910.
10. Cf. M. P. Nilsson, *Homer and Mycenae,* p. 210. London, 1933. "I should like to call this great poet Homer"; p. 265, "The distinguishing feature of Homeric poetry is the humanizing of the old and sometimes rough myths." Cf. p. 259.
11. R. Schultz, *Aidos,* pp. 4 ff. Leipzig, 1910. G. Murray, *Greek Epic,*[3] p. 327. Oxford, 1924. "Hubris is the typical sin condemned by early Greece."
12. Aristotle, *Poetics,* 1449b.
13. *Ibid.*

make the hearer shudder and pity.[14] These two emotions, fear and pity, essential to what Aristotle calls the "tragic pleasure,"[15] are evoked in the hearer or reader by the spectacle of a human being who is outraged by cruelty, whether the outrage is inflicted by decree of fate and the gods, as in the case of Oedipus and the mad Heracles, or by human ignorance and wickedness. Revulsion against cruelty is implied in Aristotle's phrase in the definition of tragedy,[16] "by means of pity and fear," and in his other references to the two emotions. As Bywater[17] says, "the apprehension [which] the tragic poet arouses in us—is a disinterested fear for another; the danger that arouses it being that of the hero, not that of the audience in the theatre."

The word *aidos*,[18] most important of the ethical words in the *Iliad*, has no exact equivalent in a single English word. It is the opposite of *hubris*, insolence, almost equally untranslatable by a single word that would cover all its meanings. Professor Gilbert Murray[19] has written some eloquent pages about *aidos*, with subtle perception of its values. He interprets *aidos* in its senses of honor, shame, reverence, and notes that in early Greek poetry it bears the meaning of "horror of cruelty or treachery toward the helpless" (p. 86), the helpless being strangers and suppliants, old people and orphan children.[20] It is a word of the older, simpler society and tends to disappear in later Greek ethics.[21] The *Iliad*

14. *Ibid.*, 1453b.
15. *Ibid.*
16. *Ibid.*, 1452a.
17. *Aristotle on the Art of Poetry*, p. 211. Oxford, 1909.
18. Cf. Aristotle, *Ethics*, 1108a, 30 ff. and 1128, 10 ff. Aristotle says that *aidos* and *nemesis* are not virtues, since they are feelings, and not the habitual attitude toward the feeling. They are, however, "means" between extremes, but "in the feelings."
19. *Greek Epic*,[3] pp. 83–91.
Cf. Schultz, *op. cit.*, pp. 6 ff.
M. Hoffmann, *Die ethische Terminologie bei Homer, Hesiod, und den alten Elegikern und Iambographen*, p. 237. Tübingen, 1914.
20. *Ibid.*, p. 87.
21. *Ibid.*, pp. 89, 90, "the virtue of a wild and ill-governed society, where there is not much effective regulation of men's actions by the law."

begins with a scene in which the Greeks show this virtue and their commander, Agamemnon, shows the opposite vice, *hubris*. Chryses, an old priest of Apollo's temple in Chryse, comes to the Greek camp to ransom his daughter Chryseis, who has been given to Agamemnon as his prize of war. The Greeks, on hearing his plea, urged Agamemnon to show *aidos* for the suppliant, to accept the ransom, and to restore the girl to her father. The war lord, instead, drove the old priest away with threats and insults. His repellent and over-bearing nature[22] and disregard of the rights of others are shown by Agamemnon both in his treatment of Chryses and in his insulting remarks to the old seer Calchas, who rightly attributed the anger of Apollo and the plague sent upon the Greek camp to Agamemnon's sin against the priest. It also appears in his treatment of Achilles, from whom he took his prize, Briseis, in recompense for Chryseis. Agamemnon is an unsympathetic character, loved by no one in the *Iliad*.

It is, perhaps, by an unconscious stroke of genius[23] that the *Iliad*, beginning with the condemnation of an act of *hubris* against an old priest, ends with an example of *aidos* shown to another old man, King Priam, to whom Achilles restores the body of his dead son, Hector. Apollo is active in both cases. In answer to Chryses' prayer he punishes the Greeks for the sin of their war lord, and, by complaining in a council of the gods that Achilles has no mercy or scruple in his heart, he starts the train of events that leads to Achilles' mercy to Priam.

The poet of the *Iliad* must have had very many *klea andron*, songs of heroes, in his memory. A verse chronicle of the Trojan War has been suggested,[24] but more probably

22. D. Mülder, *Die Ilias und ihre Quellen*, p. 297. Berlin, 1910.
"Das A hat unverkennbar die Tendenz die Handlungsweise des Agamemnon gegen Achilleus als ein himmelschreiendes Unrecht erscheinen zu lassen."
23. But cf. J. T. Sheppard, J. H. S., XL, p. 53. 1920.
24. T. W. Allen, *Homer, Origins and Transmissions*, pp. 198, 199. Oxford, 1924.

Homer knew "a nebulous mass of songs with countless variants centering about the Trojan War."[25]

Using his abundant material with the ease and freedom of creative genius he gave the poem which he composed an aesthetic and moral unity by bringing into it as its principal motivation and characteristic the spirit of *aidos*. By the entrance of this essence of the gentler virtues of the Iron Age into the verse-stuff inherited from earlier poems, the *Iliad* surpassed all that had gone before it and gained its immortality as a tragic picture of human life and human struggle.

Men of the Iron Age who listened to the recitations of the *Iliad* no doubt enjoyed the narrative of the fights about the bodies of heroes fallen on the battlefield, and took pleasure in the detailed description of the wounds, which must have formed a great part of the "songs of heroes." As William James said, their minds fed on this. But, being of that race that possessed aesthetic sensitiveness in a higher degree than any other ancient people, their minds must have fed also on the tragic beauty of the poem and on the "sense of tears in human things," so nobly expressed in it. If they laughed at Hera bickering with the king of Heaven, or cajoling him on Mt. Ida, for the benefit of her beloved Argives, they wept also with Andromache and Achilles and Priam, and came to know the "release of pity"[26] that great tragedy gives. Lucas[27] thinks that Aristotle's famous medical metaphor means that by "pity and fear" in tragedy the spectator of the hero's suffering is, temporarily at least, cured of pity and made less pitiful. I do not think that Aristotle meant that a man's *capacity* for pity is lessened by tragedy or that he is made less sensitive by sorrow for others, whether they are victims of cruelty in real life, or in the world of the poet's imagination. The "tragic pleasure,"[28] as Aristotle calls it, that comes

25. Nilsson, *Homer and Mycenae*, p. 209.
But cf. Mülder, *op. cit.*, pp. 5 f.
26. *Poetics*, 1452a.   27. F. L. Lucas, *Tragedy*, pp. 35 f. New York, 1928.
28. *Poetics*, 1453b.

through pity and fear for others makes him who experiences it more sensitive to another's pain. So Euripides taught the hearers of his plays, "struggling always not to purge them of over-pity, but to teach them more."[29] Orestes in the *Electra*[30] says: "The perception of sorrow not our own pierces the heart."

The purpose of the poet who composed the *Iliad* from old "songs of heroes" was artistic; the poem was an expression of himself and his genius, but was composed, like Shakespeare's plays, for the practical end of interesting, pleasing, and finding success with his audiences. Though, like all Greek poetry, his poem has a gnomic element, that element is slight in comparison with true didactic poetry, such as the *Works and Days*. Homer is not a preacher and Hesiod is. Homer's Zeus is not the Zeus of Aeschylus, and much of his poetry shocked Plato's[31] moral sense, always easily shocked by poetry and "Imitation." The story of the *Iliad*, the Wrath of Achilles, seems to some readers to be "of the second order,"[32] a first-rate poem on a second-rate subject.[33] Professor Murray says that, since in the loss of Briseis it is almost entirely the personal affront that matters to Achilles and not the loss of a beloved being, all the emotions are put several degrees lower. However, Achilles himself says that he loves Briseis as dearly as any faithful and loving husband loves his wife.[34] "Wrath" is a frequent motive for early epics[35] and the wrath of a man of passionate nature when a beloved woman has been taken from him, together with the slight to his honor, is not really a second-rate motive for the *Iliad*. Indeed, as Achilles himself point out, a similar occurrence in the

29. Lucas, *op. cit.*, p. 37.
30. Euripides, *Electra*, 290 f.
31. *Republic*, 377–378; 600 E.
32. J. W. Mackail, *Life of William Morris*, I, 332 f. London, 1899.
33. Murray, *Greek Epic*,[3] p. 239.
34. *Il.*, IX, 335 ff.
35. E. Bethe, *Rh. Mus.*, LXXIV (1925), "*Ilias und Meleager*," pp. 1–12; Murray, *op. cit.*, pp. 33, 184, 206; Mülder, *op. cit.*, pp. 54–56.

case of Menelaus was the cause of the expedition against Troy.

In the ninth book[36] Achilles makes a very good argument to the embassy which comes to him with Agamemnon's peace offer. He says: "He has taken my beloved wife—let him take joy in sleeping at her side! Why are the Argives fighting here at Troy? Why has Atreides gathered the troops and brought them hither? Was it not for fair-haired Helen's sake? Are the sons of Atreus the only men who love their wives? As any good and steadfast husband loves his wife and cherishes her so I loved mine with all my heart, though she was the captive of my spear." He calls Briseis his wife, ἄλοχος. The word never means concubine. That translation, given in the most recent edition of Liddell and Scott's *Dictionary* for the word in this passage and in *Od.*, IV, 623, is obviously wrong in both places. Briseis is a shadowy character but has the gentleness and beauty with which Homer endows his women. Patroclus is devoted to her and she is treated chivalrously even by Agamemnon. "Wrath" at her loss is a higher motive for the epic than quarrels about herds and cattle, the theme of many early songs.

The subject of the *Iliad* is the *effect* of the Wrath, rather than the Wrath itself. The story of the *Iliad* is the tragedy of Troy, which is also the tragedy of Achilles and of Hector. The poet who wrote the twenty-fourth book of the *Iliad*, that book of *aidos* and *eleos*—of mercy and of pity—belongs to the company of the world's greatest poets and had that wisdom of the tender-hearted, "the price of which is pain."

In the following chapter I shall consider further the question of *aidos* and *eleos* in the *Iliad* and also in the earlier poems of whose existence the *Iliad* itself gives proof.

36. *Il.*, IX, 335 ff.

II

THE GENTLER VIRTUES IN THE *ILIAD* AND
IN THE SOURCES OF THE *ILIAD*

W AS it the genius of a single poet that brought into
Greek poetry the feeling for humanity that lifted it
from a rude song to epic? Were the "songs of
heroes"[1] devoid of ethical content, celebrating only "heroic"
deeds such as the combats of chiefs, attacks on towns, and
plundering expeditions, without moralization of their
themes? To assert this would do injustice to many vanished
poems on which the spirit of Homer was nourished, which
gave him themes and inspiration. Assuredly he did not in-
vent or for the first time use the vocabulary of humane words
which appear in the *Iliad* and the *Odyssey*. This vocabulary
was inherited from past centuries, together with the Ionic
language and the hexameter verse in which the poems are
composed. Moreover, it was inevitable that Homer should
weave into his poem parts of epic, long or short, which had
been learned by him in his education in poetry.

Let us consider the ethical character of some passages that
are generally admitted to have come from older lays. One of
these is Nestor's[2] account of fighting when a young man,
which was once part of a Pylian or Ionian epic; another is
the tale of the Wrath of Meleager[3] in the ninth book, which
once belonged to an epic lay of which Meleager was the
hero.[4] Nilsson[5] holds that the Pylian epic originated among

1. *Il.*, IX, 188, 524.
2. *Ibid.*, XI, 670 ff. Mülder, *op. cit.*, pp. 281 ff.
3. *Il.*, IX, 527 ff.
4. E. Howald, "*Meleager und Achill*," *Rh. Mus.*, LXXIII (1924), 402–426.
Wilamowitz-Moellendorff, *Ilias und Homer,* pp. 217 ff. Berlin, 1920. G. Finsler,
Homer, I, 61. Leipzig, 1924.
5. *Mycenaean Origin of Greek Mythology,* p. 86. Berkeley, 1932. *Homer and
Mycenae,* p. 260. C. Robert, *Griechische Heldensage,* pp. 191, 194. Berlin, 1920.
Mülder, *op. cit.,* pp. 281 ff. Wilamowitz, *op. cit.,* p. 207.

the Pylians and migrated with them to Ionia, where parts
became incorporated in the *Iliad*. He believes that the epic
reflected a historical tradition of fighting between the Mycenaean–Pylians and tribes to the north and east.

Nestor's narrative in the eleventh book is pure exploit,
without a trace of *ethos*. He tells of his first battles, fought
in his own land.

Would I were a youth and my strength as firm as when a strife
arose between the Eleans and ourselves in a raid on cows, when
I killed Itymoneus, noble son of Hypeirochus, dweller in Elis,
while I was driving the spoil to get what was owed us. As he
defended his herds, he was struck by a spear from my hand in
the fore-front of the fighting. He fell and the folk from the
countryside were in terror around him. We drove much booty
from the plain, fifty herds of cows, as many flocks of sheep, one
hundred and twenty horses, all mares, with their foals beneath
them. We drove them to Neleian Pylos by night, to the citadel,
and the heart of Neleus rejoiced because so much spoil was mine,
though I went but a youth to the fray. And the heralds at dawn
proclaimed that all should gather who had debts owed them in
fair Elis, and the leaders of the Pylians came together and divided
the spoil, for the Epeians owed debts to many.

So he goes on, narrating the division of the spoil, the attack of the Eleans on Thryoessa, and the battle about the
citadel in which Nestor slew the first man, and then, springing upon the fleeing Epeians like a black tempest, captured
fifty chariots and killed one hundred men. He killed the last
man of the enemy at Bouprasium and drove back to Pylos
with his comrades, where all gave praise to Zeus and to
Nestor.

The tale is written in the "great metre" and in the fine
epic language, but in spirit it is as primitive as the songs of
those other border men who "drove the beeves of Lauder-
dale."

The story of the Wrath of Meleager, told by old Phoenix
in order to persuade Achilles to accept the gifts offered by
Agamemnon and be reconciled to him, has been thought to
be the original story of *Menis* (wrath) that suggested the mo-

tive of the *Iliad* and the direful Wrath of Achilles. Bethe,[6] while denying this influence and maintaining that the Meleager epic is not old, admits that it was older than the ninth book of the *Iliad*. He calls the author of the saga used by Phoenix "that gifted poet, whom Phoenix follows in his speech" (p. 7). Phoenix himself says that his tale is "one of long ago and not of yesterday."

He omits the death of Meleager from his tale, which he chooses from old "songs of heroes" (v. 524) to point a moral for Achilles by telling him of another of the many heroes who, though overcome by furious anger, yet in return for gifts gave up their wrath. The parallel between Meleager and Achilles is artificial[7] and Phoenix does not set it forth very skilfully. The tale as told here is this. Artemis was enraged with Oeneus, king of Aetolia, because he did not offer her the first fruits of the harvest. She sent a wild boar to ravage the vineyards. Meleager, son of Oeneus, at the head of huntsmen and hounds killed the wild boar. The goddess, still angry, set the Kouretes and Aetolians to fighting for the boar's head and hide. What follows is told with gaps in the story. Meleager fought with and drove back the Kouretes. "Anger, that swells in the breast of many a man, though he be wise of heart, overcame Meleager, and enraged with his mother Althaea, he lay at the side of his wedded wife, Cleopatra," angered because of his mother's curses. His mother was grief-stricken because of her brother's death. (He was one of the Kouretes and slain by Meleager.) She beat upon the earth, calling upon Hades and Persephone to give her son to death; Erinys, who walks in darkness, with pitiless heart, heard her. Nothing is told about the fateful brand, the burning of which brought death to Meleager. Only the story of his Wrath is useful for the aim of Phoenix and he continues with the tale of that. The noise of the foe and the

6. Bethe, *Rh. Mus.*, LXXIV (1925), *"Ilias und Meleager,"* p. 9.
7. Mülder, *op. cit.*, pp. 49 ff., 54–56.
Murray, *Greek Epic*,[3] pp. 181 ff.

din of battering-rams resounded about the citadel where Meleager and Cleopatra lay. The councilors sent priests to beseech him to come forth and fight, offering him the best of the ploughland and vineland of lovely Calydon. His father, his sisters, and his mother came and his dearest and most faithful comrades. He refused them all and would not yield until his very chamber door was battered and the Kouretes were climbing on the towers and setting fire to the town. Then his wife besought him to go forth, telling him of all the woe that comes to those whose city is captured—the men are slain, the town laid waste with fire, the children and women are taken into captivity. Meleager's soul was stirred as he heard these evil things. He put on his armor and went forth and saved the Aetolians, but they did not give him the gifts they had promised, though he drove destruction from them. The story of his death is not told by Phoenix, as that would be a bad omen for Achilles.

Phoenix concludes his speech by begging Achilles to accept gifts offered by Agamemnon and to come back to the fighting. If he comes for the gifts, the Achaeans will honor him as a god, but if he enters the battle without taking the gifts, he will not have the same honor, even if he shall turn the tide of battle.

The lay of Meleager appears here in a much-shortened form, adapted to the hoped-for effect on Achilles.

The poets and artists of Greece and Rome found the saga of Meleager an inexhaustible source of inspiration for their work. Its themes are repeated by tragedians, by sculptors, and vase painters, and appear on many varied works of art, Etruscan urns, Roman sarcophagi, mosaics, gems, and other representative monuments. Aristotle[8] names the tragic story of Meleager as one of those employed for the plots of the finest tragedies. We know that Phrynichus[9] dramatized the

8. *Poetics*, 1453a.
9. Paus. X, 31, 4.
C. Robert, *Hermes*, XXXIV, pp. 153 ff. 1898.

story in his *Women of Pleuron* and both Sophocles and Euripides wrote tragedies entitled *Meleagros*. Of the Sophoclean drama nothing remains, but the statement is made by Pliny[10] that, in the play, after Meleager's death his weeping sisters were transported to India and beyond and changed into guinea fowl, dropping tears of amber from their eyes. Ovid found this metamorphosis very useful.[11] Euripides' play must have been one of his most pathetic and, as Robert[12] says, gave the saga its final form, which so greatly influenced the art of Scopas in the pediments of the temple of Alea at Tegea, the artists of the frieze of Gjölbaschi, and the vases of the fourth century.[13] Several fragments of the *Meleagros* of Euripides are extant and Apollodorus[14] gives a résumé of it. Its continuing tragic power is seen in Swinburne's early beautiful drama, *Atalanta in Calydon,* called by Harold Nicolson "the most valuable as well as the most communicable of all Swinburne's work."[15] Swinburne takes one of the Euripidean fragments as the motto for his poem.

> Help thou the living. Every man when dead
> Is earth and shadow, naught that goes to naught.[16]

In the sixth century the Calydonian Boar hunt was sung by Stesichorus[17] and painted on the François vase and on other black-figured vases. In the fifth century the theme of the most beautiful of the odes of Bacchylides[18] is the meeting in Hades of Heracles and the shade of Meleager, who tells him of his death, when the "brand of speedy doom" was burned by his mother, angered because of the death of her two brothers, whom Meleager had slain in fair fight, "for the

10. Pliny, *N. H.,* XXXVII, 40.
11. Ovid, *Met.,* VII, 533 ff.
12. *Die Griechische Heldensage,* I, 98.
13. *Ibid.,* pp. 97 f.
14. *Bibliotheca,* I, 8, 2 ff.
15. H. Nicolson, *Swinburne,* p. 92. London, 1926.
16. My translation.
17. Athenaeus III, 95, d.
18. *Ode* V.

passionate War-god makes no distinction in battle between kinsmen and men of other blood, and arrows go blindly from the hand against the lives of the enemy."[19] The story is told with Bacchylides' characteristic pathos and exquisite decorative language. Swinburne, of course, knew nothing of it, since the papyrus containing the poems of Bacchylides was not discovered until 1896, but his poem and that of Bacchylides have the same melancholy beauty.

In the ode of Bacchylides Meleager says: "It chanced that I was slaying Clymenus, the gallant son of Daipylus in front of the wall where I had found him, a glorious warrior—our foes were in flight to the fair-lying ancient city of Pleuron—when sweet life ebbed within me and I knew that my strength was waning.[20] Alas! as I drew my last breath, I wept for my fate in leaving so soon my splendid youth." The poem continues: "It is said that for the first time the eyes of Heracles were wet with tears, in pity for the sorrowful hero's fate, and he answered him with these words: 'Best for mortals never to have been born and looked upon the sunlight.'"

The poem of Bacchylides is believed to have derived from the drama of Phrynichus, the *Women of Pleuron*, mentioned by Pausanias,[21] who quotes these verses from the chorus of that play: "He did not escape chill death. A swift flame of the brand burned by his dread mischievous mother destroyed him."

Phrynichus evidently knew and used the form of the saga which had the story of the brand. Phoenix in the *Iliad* purposely and obviously suppresses the death of Meleager, so that it is impossible to know whether the saga which he

---

19. *Vv.* 129 ff.
20. Compare *Atlanta in Calydon,*
    "He wastes as the embers quicken,
    "With the brand he fades as a brand."
Also, Euripides, *Frag.* 971.
"In the bloom of his strength and beauty, his light went out, like a falling star."
21. X, 31.
Robert, *Hermes,* XXIX, pp. 130–159. 1898.

quotes had Meleager die in battle with the Kouretes, slain
by Apollo,[22] or told the story of the fateful brand, burned
by his mother. Whichever is the fact (and most scholars
believe that the brand *motif* was a very early one), there
exists in both accounts the tragic motive of anger between
mother and son. The anger of Althaea in the *Iliad* is much
more powerful and grim than that of her son. Though
Phoenix intentionally refrains from telling the result, the
situation in any case is the one so potent in Greek tragedy,
in which "the incidents are most productive of pity or
fear";[23] that is, "when the tragic deed is done within the
family, when brother slays brother, or son his father, or
mother her son, or son his mother."

The elements of tragedy, therefore, were in the old pre-
Homeric epic in the "family-drama" of Althaea and her son.
The old epic will not have had the tender beauty of the ode
of Bacchylides, nor the conscious pathos of Euripides, but
pity and fear entered into it, and if we may judge from the
extraordinary influence which it exercised on the poetry and
art of all the following centuries down into the Roman period, it was a lay of great tragic power. It is notable that in
the form of the story found in the *Iliad* Meleager is per-
suaded to defend his city by his wife's telling him of the
sufferings that come on noncombatants in a captured city.
The words describe what the Greek world knew well from
the bitter experiences of countless wars. Aeschylus gives the
same description in his own words in the *Seven against
Thebes*.[24] The sufferings are made real also in the play[25]
which Euripides placed on the stage in order that his fellow-
citizens might behold the savagery of such a war as they
themselves had waged the year before against Melos.

The story of Meleager and his mother's anger, which be-

22. Hesiod, *Eoeae, ap.* Paus. X, 31, 3.
Apollodorus, *Bibliotheca,* I, 72.
23. Aristotle, *Poetics,* 1453a.
24. *Septem,* 321 ff.
25. *The Trojan Women,* produced 415 B.C.

longs to ancient folk tale[26] and to pre-Homeric saga, is clear
proof that the old myths had already been humanized before
they were used by Homer. The sympathetic treatment of the
two Lycian heroes, Glaucus and the great Sarpedon, the son
of Zeus, the delightful example of chivalry and courtesy[27]
on the battlefield when the two combatants, Glaucus and
Diomede, on finding that their forebears have been friends,
exchange armor instead of fighting, the touching narrative
of the death of Sarpedon[28] and the sorrow of Glaucus for
him, the romantic adventures of Bellerophon[29] in Lycia, told
by his grandson Glaucus—all suggest that there existed
"Lycian" epics,[30] celebrating fights of the Lycians and
Greeks, which already had humane *traits*.

Homer's vocabulary of humane words was inherited by
him from earlier poets and must have had a long history.
Certain recurring familiar lines in which such words occur
were, in all likelihood, taken from lays which the poet knew
and from whose influence he could not escape. I will give
examples of these words which occur in the *Iliad* and the
Odyssey with no appearance of novelty.

The word *aidos,* shame, regard for others, what a man's
conscience demands of him, I have already discussed in the
first chapter. This word[31] is joined with *eleos,* pity, in Apollo's indictment of Achilles' cruelty.

"So Achilles has lost pity and no shame enters his heart,
shame that is a great hurt and a great help to a man."

This is the only instance of the word *eleos* in the Homeric
poems. Another word, *oiktos,* appears in the *Odyssey* in a
formula twice employed—"pity seized," the object in one

26. E. Kuhnert, *Rh. Mus.* XLIX (1894), p. 57.

27. *Il.,* VI, 119 ff.

28. *Ibid*, XVI, 419 ff.

29. *Ibid.,* VI, 155 ff.

30.   Nilsson, *Homer and Mycenae,* pp. 261–263.
Mülder, *op. cit.,* p. 92. Cf. p. 98, for the "Rhodian-Lycian epos" and
Sarpedon and Glaucus.

31. *Il.,* XXIV, 43–44. The second line is found in Hesiod, *Works and Days,*
317.

case being "all the folk" (*Od.*, II, 81), in the other "all the Achaeans" (*Od.*, XXIV, 438).

It is remarkable that the Homeric language is so shy of the two nouns, for the verbs and adjectives derived from them occur frequently.

The second of the two words, *oiktos,* is the more usual in later Greek. It is the word for pity used by Euripides in the verses about pity in the *Electra.* The word ἐλεητύς appears twice[32] in the *Odyssey,* in both cases referring to those who have no ruth in taking or giving freely of the goods of others; it refers to the suitors eating the best of the swine "without ruth," and Antinous uses it in the same way about giving the good of others "without ruth" to shameless beggars. It has a weakened meaning here and does not occur elsewhere. The verb ἐλεέω occurs twenty-seven times in the *Iliad,* much less often in the *Odyssey,* while οἰκτίρω, with the same meaning, is found five times in the *Iliad* and not at all in the *Odyssey.* The verb ἐλεαίρω, pity, occurs about a dozen times in each poem. ἐλεήμων,[33] pitiful, merciful, occurs once in the Odyssey. The adjective οἰκτρός has one example in the *Iliad,* several, usually adverbial neuter plural, in the *Odyssey;* ἐλεεινός, pitiable, appears in both poems, more frequently in the *Iliad.* The adjective νηλής, pitiless, describes the unrelenting Achilles in the *Iliad,*[34] and often the large cutting tool of war, the sword, in the phrase, "with the pitiless bronze." This phrase is echoed in the *Odyssey,* where firewood[35] is split "with the pitiless bronze." In the *Iliad* the phrase occurs in battle scenes or in the ritual killing of sacrificial victims. The "pitiless day" of death is a recurring phrase, of which there are seven instances in the *Iliad,* two in the *Odyssey.*

The distribution of the words for mercy and pity in the *Iliad* and *Odyssey* is not of great significance, but the con-

---

32. *Od.,* XIV, 82; XVII, 451 (not in the *Iliad*).
33. *Ibid.,* V, 191.
34. *Il.,* IX, 632.
35. *Od.,* XIV, 418.

text in which the words appear indicates that pity enters
more fully into the texture of the *Iliad*. This is but natual,
since the *Iliad* is the tragic poem. Yet the *Odyssey*, though a
"comedy of characters," has many pathetic scenes and contains the exquisitely melancholy Book of the Dead,[36] the
Nekuia.

Among the inheritances from older lays I would count the
line that is used in the *Iliad* to link together battle scenes and
to motivate combats between the heroes. The warrior, "seeing his comrade fallen, is moved to pity." So he strikes down
a foe in vengeance for his friend or tribesman. The poet uses
the line to carry on the dramatic description of the fighting
and to enrich with personal feeling the monotonous cata-
logue of duels between Greek and Trojan.

The formula first appears in *Il.*, V, 561. Menelaus perceives that the two sons of Diocles have been slain by Aeneas.
"He pitied them fallen and went through the foremost ranks,
equipped with gleaming bronze, shaking his spear." With
the help of Antilochus he killed Pylaemenes, a Paphlagonian
prince. A little further on in the same book the line comes
again with the dual object, with Telamonian Ajax as subject.
He is moved with pity for the victims of Hector's spear and
to avenge them kills Amphios, an ally of Priam. In the seven-
teenth book the line carries on the tale of fighting. Lycome-
don[37] pities Leiocritus, wounded by Aeneas, and strikes down
Apisaon, a Paeonian ally of the Trojans. When Apisaon fell,
mortally wounded, Prince Asteropaeus pitied him and made
a fruitless attempt to recover the dead body of his friend and
countryman and to avenge him.

The verb οἰκτίρω, to pity, appears twice in a similar verse,
with Achilles as its subject, once[38] at the beginning of the
sixteenth book, when Patroclus comes to Achilles, weeping,
and "Achilles, seeing him, was stirred with pity." Again,[39]

36. The eleventh book of the *Odyssey*.
37. *Il.*, XVII, 346 ff.
38. *Ibid.*, XVI, 5.
39. *Ibid.*, XXIII, 534.

in the twenty-third book, Achilles pities Eumelus, who comes in last in the chariot race.

The word ἐλέησε, pitied, finds a place in the wonderful farewell of Hector going to battle and Andromache. Hector had dandled and kissed their child after the babe's dismay at his father's gleaming bronze armor and horsehair crest, and had prayed that the infant should become a mightier warrior than his father, should return from battle victorious, and gladden his mother's heart. Andromache then took the child, "laughing through her tears." Her husband was filled with pity as he looked.[40]

The other verb from ἔλεος, ἐλεαίρω, to pity, commonly appears in a negative statement at the end of a verse. An example is Andromache's appeal to Hector.[41]
"Perverse one, your daring will be your ruin and you have no pity," etc. (cf. *Il.*, VII, 27; X, 176; XI, 665).

Joined with κήδεται, ἐλεαίρω several times has Zeus for its subject, in the line "who, though far away, cares for you and pities you."

The formula "saw and pitied" has Hera as subject in *Il.*, VIII, 350. She saw and pitied the Greeks pursued by Hector. Zeus[42] saw and pitied the horses of Achilles, as they stood still, mourning for their driver Patroclus, afar from the battle.

I suspect that these imbedded formulae were found in earlier epic. Others that have the same function in adding a dramatic touch to the dull narrative of fighting are those in which ἄχος, grief, and ἀχνύμενος, grieved, are found. In *Iliad*, VIII, 124,[43] "Grief for his charioteer darkened the heart of Hector." The words ὀλοφύρομαι, to lament for (cf. *Il.*, XXII, 169 f.) and κήδομαι (cf. *Il.*, I, 56) are used in the sense of pity. A scholiast explains the former of these verbs by the two words for pity.

40. *Ibid.*, VI, 484.
41. *Ibid.*, 405.
42. *Ibid.*, XVII, 441.
43. Also in *ibid.*, XVII, 83 ff. Cf. also *ibid.*, XIII, 581; XIV, 475; XVI, 581.

The word "pitied" in the formula used in descriptions of battle signifies pity for one of the same tribe or family and is joined to lust for vengeance and hatred of the enemy. After Sarpedon's death Hector's rush upon the enemy is motivated in the Greek, not by "pity for Sarpedon," but by "rage because of Sarpedon."[44]

This tribal pity is felt by the fierce goddess Hera for her Argives, while for the Trojans she has such hatred that Zeus tells her she would be glad "to enter the gates of Troy and eat raw Priam, his children and the other Trojans."[45] Hera is the personification of racial hatred and narrow love of her own tribe. Athena is her second, acting under her orders (cf. *Il.*, I, 208 ff., V, 719; VIII, 351, 457 ff.; XI, 45, etc.). Her hatred of the Trojans is as bitter as that of Hera, whereas Zeus has a regard for both Greeks and Trojans and is on his way to become the truly catholic god to whom the noble *Hymn of Cleanthes* is addressed. Although in war "Pity's sleeping," pity for the enemy is not unknown in the battles of the *Iliad*. Menelaus[46] has the impulse to spare Adrestus, who kneels before him, begging for his life and offering ransom. He is checked, however, by Agamemnon, who utters the most shocking expression of hate to be found in the *Iliad*. "Soft Menelaus, why have you such pity for the foe? Has your home reaped so many blessings from the Trojans? May no one of them escape sheer death at our hands, even if it be the man-child that his mother carries in her womb. May all in Ilium perish unburied and unknown." The episode is one of the pathetic scenes on the battlefield which abound in the *Iliad*. Sympathy is with the suppliant Adrestus and with Menelaus and against the brutality of Agamemnon who here, as elsewhere in the *Iliad*, is, in the words of the Chorus in the *Agamemnon* of Aeschylus, "painted in no lovely light."[47]

But to our dismay the epic story continues in a way that

44. *Ibid.*, XVI, 553.
45. *Ibid.*, IV, 33–36.
46. *Ibid.*, VI, 45 ff.
47. *Ag.*, 801.

has caused great distress to commentators: "With these words he diverted the heart of his brother from his purpose, giving him *just counsel*." Thus the poet commends Agamemnon's monstrous words of cruelty. I do not approve of a change of αἴσιμα (just) to αἴσυλα (unjust), nor do I agree with Miss Stawell's[48] argument that παρειπών in this passage and in *Il.*, VII, 121, means "uttering awry," "perverting the right." The phrase αἴσιμα παρειπών appears to me to be an "unexpurgated" phrase, left over from an older lay, perhaps used here carelessly for "giving him timely advice"; i.e., just in time to prevent Menelaus from yielding to his impulse of mercy.

Nowhere else does the *Iliad* praise cruelty, except in the tenth book, the *Doloneia,* which is regarded by most scholars as later than the rest of the *Iliad*. I shall discuss this book in my next chapter.

Unlike Agamemnon, Achilles is naturally inclined to mercy. He tells Lycaon,[49] Priam's son, whose life he had once spared, that before Patroclus was killed he preferred not to kill the Trojans, but that now he is merciless, because of his friend's death. It is a wonderful and terrible speech that he makes to the trembling Trojan—"Fool! proffer me no ransom, nor plead to me. Before Patroclus met his fatal day, it was my pleasure rather to spare the Trojans and I took many captive and sold them in the isles. But now there is not one who shall escape death, if a god puts any in my hands before the walls of Troy, not one of all the Trojans, and above all, no son of Priam. My friend, die also. Why thus bewail? Patroclus died, a better man than you. Look you how tall and fine a man I am. My sire was noble, my mother is a goddess. But death and crushing fate await me too. The dawn shall come, or evening, or high noon when one shall take my life in battle by a spear's cast, or by an arrow from his bowstring."

48. F. M. Stawell, *Homer and the Iliad,* p. 29. London, 1909.
49. *Il.*, XXI, 96 ff.

Though Achilles feels that he owes the life of every Trojan to the spirit of Patroclus, these are not the words of a man who delights in killing, but rather of one who is obsessed with the idea of exacting the *poine*,[50] the blood penalty for his friend. He apologizes[51] to the dead Patroclus for his act of *aidos* in restoring Hector's body to his father.

Agamemnon's relentless spirit and his greed[52] are illustrated in *Il.*, XI, 101 ff. in contrast with the generous and merciful spirit of Achilles. He killed and stripped of their splendid armor two sons of Priam, whom Achilles had once caught on Ida tending the flocks, and had set them free for ransom. Agamemnon knew their armor, for he had marked it well as they came down from Ida with Achilles. He justifies Achilles' taunt of covetousness.

In *Troilus and Cressida*[53] young Troilus, maddened by Cressida's treachery, reproaches Hector for his mercy to the Greeks in lines that are a distant parallel to Agamemnon's reproach of Menelaus for his softness.

Tro. Brother, you have a vice of mercy in you
    Which better fits a lion than a man.
Hect. What vice is that, good Troilus? Chide me for it.
Tro. When many times the captive Grecians fall,
    Even in the face and wind of your fair sword,
    You bid them rise and live.
Hect. O 'tis fair play.
Tro. Fool's play, by Heaven, Hector.
Hect. How now! how now!
Tro.   For the love of all the gods,
    Let's leave the hermit pity with our mothers;
    And when we have our armours buckled on,
    The venomed vengeance ride upon our swords;
    Spur them to ruthful work, rein them from ruth.
Hect. Fie, savage, fie!
Tro. Hector, then 'tis wars.

50. *Ibid.*, XIV, 482–485.
51. *Ibid.*, XXIV, 593–595.
52. Cf. *Ibid.*, I, 122, 149, 163 ff.
53. Act V, Scene III.

Achilles, whose heart can be touched to mercy, is still a child of the Early Iron Age (I speak of the period of the poet who took the Wrath of Achilles for his theme) and must be judged by the standards of that age and of the rules of warfare prevailing in that time. It seems unchivalrous to us[54] that Achilles always takes the ransom for his prisoners, as Agamemnon accepts the ransom for Chryseis. Phoenix says in the ninth book of the *Iliad* that it would be dishonorable for Achilles to come back to the battlefield without receiving the gifts sent to bribe him to come. He must come for the gifts, or he will not be honored by the Greeks. Moreover, Achilles' treatment of Hector's body, his rough speech[55] to old King Priam combined with his tenderness to him,[56] belong to a character conceived by a very great poet of an age not our own. That poet understands Achilles and makes him intelligible to us. He understands the wild savagery of war and in the midst of his narrative of its bloody combats he tells in a few poignant words of the tragedy of the young men, Greek, or Trojan ally, who die far from home and all who love them.

There is Iphidamas,[57] who had come from Thrace, straight from his bridal chamber, and was killed by Agamemnon.

"And so he fell and slept the sleep of bronze, a pitiable man, far from his wedded wife, fighting for Troy, far from his bride, whose loveliness he knew not, and he gave a great dowry for her."

The sorrow of those who mourn at home for the dead, sung in the marvelous chorus[58] of Aeschylus, is pictured by a bitterly taunting enemy in the fourteenth book.[59]

"I pray you, Trojans, bid the loving father and mother of

54. As it did to Plato, *Republic*, 390 E.
55. *Il.*, XXIV, 559–570.
56. *Ibid.*, 515 ff.
57. *Ibid.*, XI., 221 ff.
58. *Ag.*, 433–436.
59. *Il.*, XIV, 501 ff.

proud Ilioneus to weep in their halls, for neither shall the wife of Agenor's son, Promachus, take joy in her dear husband's return to her, when we young men of the Achaeans sail home from Troy."

The tenderness of the poet appears in a simile in the eighth book, a book which one critic[60] rejects altogether as a late addition and another calls "perhaps the least satisfying book of the *Iliad*."[61] It is the loveliest simile in the *Iliad*.[62] Gorgythion, son of Priam and fair Kastianeira, was struck in the breast by Teucer's arrow, aimed at Hector. "As a poppy in the garden, when its cup is heavy with seeds and the rain-drops of the spring, droops its head, so his head drooped, beneath the burden of his helmet." These are lines of imperishable beauty, which Virgil felt and adapted in one of his most Virgilian passages.[63]

> *volvitur Euryalus leto, pulchrosque per artus*
> *it cruor, inque humeros cervix collapsa recumbit.*
> *purpureus veluti cum flos succisus aratro*
> *languescit moriens, lassove papavera collo*
> *demisere caput, pluvia cum forte gravantur.*

The description of the young Gorgythion and the poppy simile illustrates what Bowra[64] so well says of Homer's similes: "His genius compelled him to write of the heroic past and to it he devoted his majestic powers, but he knew too of the immediate present, and this he celebrated in his similes, spending his great tenderness and love of simple things in these adornments for his heroic tale."

With all the discussion[65] that has been carried on about

60. Stawell, *op. cit.*, pp. 31, 236.

61. T. W. Allen, *Homer, Origins and Transmissions*, p. 109.

62. *Il.*, VIII, 306–308.   63. *Aen.*, IX, 433.

64. C. M. Bowra, *Traditions and Design in the Iliad*, pp. 127–128. Oxford, 1930.

65. Cf., among many others, Mülder, *Die Ilias und ihre Quellen*, p. 329; Murray, *Greek Epic*[3], pp. 245 ff.; E. Drerup, *Homerische Poetik*, I, 457 ff. (Würzburg, 1921); Bowra, *op. cit.*, pp. 114 ff.; Nilsson, *Homer and Mycenae*, pp. 275 ff.

the Homeric similes, it has not been possible to decide with certainty which of them had been used before Homer. Whether they are adapted to the context exactly or not, at least the choice of them is his, as well as the invention, in all likelihood, of the freshest and most vivid of them. Similes must have found a place in earlier poems known to Homer. He could not have invented this feature of his style, though he probably largely extended the use of such comparisons.

I will mention one more simile of the poppy,[66] the only other comparison, I think, to a flower in the *Iliad*.[67] This time it is grim and horrible, not tender and lovely. In the fierce and relentless tribal fighting described at the end of the fourteenth book, the Boeotian Peneleos sent his spear through the eye of Ilioneus, cleft off his head with his sword, and held it up on the spear "like a poppy-head," brandishing it before the Trojans with ugly taunts which the poet has filled with tragic pity. The baleful flower heightens the horror of the awful scene.

Many of the tenderest of these similes refer to a young Trojan who has fallen.[68] In the fourth book of the *Iliad*[69] Simoeisios falls,

a strong youth whom his mother bore by the banks of Simoeis when she came down from Ida, following her parents to see the flocks. So they called their son Simoeisios. He did not pay his dear parents the cost of his upbringing, for his life was brief— he was laid low by the spear of bold-hearted Ajax. Through his shoulder the bronze spear went and he fell to earth like a poplar tree, which grows smooth in the low ground in a great marsh; a wainwright felled it with gleaming iron, that he might make a felloe for a fine chariot, and it lies drying by the river-bank. Such was Simoeisios, Anthemon's son, whom Ajax slew.

66. *Il.* XIV, 499.
67. But cf. *Il.*, XVII, 56, where a fallen Trojan youth is compared to a young olive tree full of white blossoms, uprooted by a whirlwind.
68. Yet H. M. Chadwick says (*The Heroic Age*, p. 179, Cambridge, 1912) that the point of view throughout the *Iliad* is that of an Achaean.
69. *Il.*, IV, 474 ff.

The highly developed simile here gives a beautiful picture taken from everyday life. The iron tool used to fell the poplar betrays the Iron Age. This simile, one thinks, must be one of Homer's own inventions, used to lend pathos and variety to the tale of the young Trojan's death. Bowra[70] has noted that similes occur chiefly in books where there is hardly anything but fighting.

One of the most charming of the shorter similes is that which Achilles uses in the scene at the beginning of the sixteenth book.[71] "Why are you so steeped in tears, Patroclus, like a little girl, running at her mother's side, begging to be taken in her arms, tugging at her dress, holding her back from her errand, and looking at her with tears until she takes her up?" Such a tenderly playful simile is appropriate on Achilles' lips, as it would not be on the lips of any other of the Greek heroes.

Thus the similes add humanity and tenderness to the grim story of the Bronze Age warfare.

I have tried to make it clear that it is by no means likely or possible that no poets before Homer wrote of merciful deeds and humane emotions and that the very vocabulary of Homer forbids this assumption. Homer's superiority and greatness results from genius and an understanding of the hearts of men which is able to interpret them in a dramatic poem, filled with the sense of the beauty of the quality of mercy.

There is a scene in the twenty-second book of the *Iliad*[72] full of horrid cruelty, in which the chiefs of the Achaeans gloat over the body of Hector. After Achilles had drawn the spear from the body and made plunder of the blood-stained armor, "the other chiefs came close and looked with wonder on the noble form and face of Hector, and each one pricked him with his spear, saying one to another

70. Bowra, *op. cit.*, p. 123.
71. *Il.*, XVI, 7–10.
72. *Ibid.*, XXII, 369 ff.

'Ah! Hector now is softer to the touch than when he burned our ships with blazing fire'—so each one spoke and came close and made his wound."

The Achaeans gloat and the poet tells of it, but the poet does not share their gloating. The book is the "Death of Hector," rather than the "Triumph of Achilles," and to talk of "our exultation with Achilles"[73] is to miss the meaning of the tragic poet of the *Iliad* and to fall far short of his humanity. The book ends with the wailing of Andromache and the Trojan women for Hector. Homer does not "exult" with Achilles.

If the poet gloated as the Achaeans gloat,[74] the scene would be as revolting and unfit for tragedy as the scalping exploits of a red Indian, or an exultant, sadistic account of a lynching. But the poet who tells of the savagery of the Achaean chiefs—it may be a fragment left over from a crude earlier lay—tells it as part of the tragic fate of Hector, with whose burial in the midst of mourning the *Iliad* closes.

In the next chapter I discuss the *Doloneia*, the tenth book of the *Iliad*, a book untouched by *aidos*.

73. Stawell, *op. cit.*, p. 78.
74. Compare the scenes of repeated stabbings in Shakespeare, *Henry VI*, pt. 3, I, 4; V, 5.

III

RUTHLESSNESS IN THE DOLONEIA AND PITY IN THE RHESUS

The Doloneia

THE tenth book of the *Iliad* has the appearance of being a separate lay, unconnected with the preceding and the following books. There is evidence that it was so regarded in early times[1] and many scholars of today believe that it does not suit the tone of the rest of the *Iliad,* but is, as Nilsson calls it, a notorious addition,[2] composed by a late minstrel.[3] Various points of language and style seem to indicate a later date for the *Doloneia.* I shall not, however, discuss these, as they do not concern the point of which this chapter treats; that is, the shamelessness with which the exploit narrated in this book is told. It is a book without *aidos,* the striking characteristic of the Iliad. Those who defend the book as Homeric, and as much a part of the *Iliad* as any other book, maintain that the departure from the heroic ideal of conduct in the book is no greater than that of Agamemnon in the first book, or that indicated in various speeches of heroes, such as those of Patroclus in *Il.,* XVI, 559, 745 ff. It is argued in defense of the *Doloneia* that Homer does not make his heroes perfect and that in general the heroic ideal of ethics is not high. This defense misses the point that it is the moral outlook of the poet himself and not the ethics of his characters that determines the standard of the poem. True, the poet of the *Iliad* does not make his heroes perfect, but he does not praise or show himself in sympathy

1. Murray, *Greek Epic*[3], pp. 158 ff., 296.
2. Nilsson, *Homer and Mycenae,* p. 159.
3. *Ibid.,* p. 260. Wilamowitz-Moellendorff, *op. cit.,* pp. 60 ff. Cf. p. 61, "Es gab die Ilias, gab auch eine Odysee, als dies Einzelgedicht verfasst ward."

with their cruel and treacherous acts. As I have abundantly shown, he has tenderness and sympathy for both Greeks and Trojans, for Glaucus and Sarpedon and Hector as well as for Patroclus and Achilles, and he does not take delight in cruelty and *hubris*.

Those who accept the *Doloneia* as an integral part of the *Iliad* either consider it a gay and joyous interlude between the defeat of the Greeks in the ninth book and their renewed efforts in the eleventh,[4] or else as a grim and bloody book, suited to its context.[5]

The *Doloneia* sets itself off from the rest of the *Iliad* by its unchivalrous spirit and its rejoicing over a deed which consists in the murder of sleeping men and their king by two of the most conspicuous heroes of the *Iliad,* who earlier in the book have killed the spy Dolon (they themselves are spies), after he had received from one of them assurance of being spared. There is only one passage[6] in which the plight of the murdered Thracians is viewed from the side of the victims, that in which Apollo awakes Hippokoon, cousin of the Thracian king. Hippokoon looks upon the men gasping in the death struggle and moans for his beloved friend and comrade. Other than this there is no trace of sympathy for the slain soldiers. The words *aidomenos* and *aidos* occur[7] (once each) in the tenth book, but in the weaker meaning of respect for rank. Ruth and pity, which make the rest of the *Iliad* "a profoundly moral story,"[8] are conspicuously absent from the *Doloneia*.

The action of the book occupies one night. Agamemnon and Menelaus are troubled by fears of a night attack and, being unable to sleep, they go to seek counsel from Nestor, who arouses Odysseus and Diomede. They go on to find the other kings of the Argives and hold a council. Diomede

---

4. A. Shewan, *The Lay of Dolon*, pp. 7–10. London, 1911.
5. Allen, *op. cit.*, p. 193.
6. *Il.*, X, 515–525.
7. *Ibid.*, X, 237–238.
8. Bowra, *op. cit.*, p. 26.

volunteers to go to the camp of the Trojans to spy out what is happening there and chooses Odysseus for his comrade.

A similar scene was enacted in Troy. Hector summons a council of the chiefs and calls for a volunteer to go to the Greek camp to find out whether the ships are guarded, or whether the Greeks are planning to sail back home under cover of night. A wealthy Trojan named Dolon offers to go to the ship of Agamemnon, where the chiefs are likely to hold a council, and spy out all. He is characterized as ugly to look upon, but a swift runner. An unfavorable impression of him is given from the time of his entrance on the scene, in contrast to the praises given to the two Greek spies, Diomede and Odysseus. Dolon's weak character is suggested by the fact that he is the only son brought up with five sisters and his covetousness by his demand that Hector give him the chariot and horses of Achilles for his reward. Promised these by Hector, he put on a gray wolf-skin and a ferret-skin helmet and went on his way to the ships. "But he was not destined to come back from the ships to report to Hector." A peculiarity of the book is the description of the beasts' skins which the heroes put on. Agamemnon and Diomede arrayed themselves in long red lion skins, reaching to the feet, Menelaus put on a spotted leopard's skin. And Odysseus, to the delight of archaeologists,[9] wore a helmet of leather having many straps within it; on the outside gleaming white teeth of a boar were set on either side. This was an heirloom with a long history, lent by Meriones, the Cretan, to Odysseus.

Dolon is seen by the Greek chiefs, who chase and catch him, trembling and "green with fear." He begs for life, promising them a great ransom. Odysseus bids him take courage and not to worry about death, but rather tell them why he is wandering alone among the ships. Dolon tells them how he came to spy on the Greeks, induced by Hector's promise to give him the famous divine horses of Achilles

if he should succeed in his task. The smiling Odysseus asks
him how the Trojan guards are posted, where Hector and
his horses are, and what the Trojans have in mind to do.
Full information is given by Dolon, who adds the fact that
King Rhesus has arrived from Thrace in his gold and
silver chariot drawn by snow-white horses, and that he and
his Thracian soldiers are sleeping at a distance from the
other Trojan allies. On learning this valuable piece of news
Diomede responds to Dolon's plea for life by cutting off his
head. The two Greeks then stripped the body of the wolf
skin and the helmet and his bow and spear, to be kept as
an offering to Athena.

They then went on to their work of killing the sleeping
Thracians. "And the perpetrators of the deed are away
with the famous team, merry over the success of their
escapade. . . . As for the scout . . . he is lying on the
plain naked and headless, dear to the dogs and vultures,
while his fellows are howling in panic about the corpses
of the Thracians, while Odysseus and Diomede are enjoying
the welcome of their friends."[10] This is not the tone of
the poet of the *Iliad*. I have quoted this exultant description of the exploit of the two Greeks from a critic who
sees in it a gay story full of "healthy freshness" and "intense
enjoyment of life."[11] In one respect his words do injustice
to the *Doloneia*. I have already referred to the grief of
Hippokoon (v. 552) for his beloved friend. This is interpreted "his fellows are howling in pain," etc. The whole
discussion[12] in its bitterness and sarcasm against Hector
shows this critic to be far more "Achaean"[13] than Homer.

The horrid scene of the slaughter of the Thracians has
no condemnation from the poet. The butcher Diomede
slays on this side and on that, until he has killed twelve

10. Shewan, *op. cit.*, p. 7.
11. *Ibid.*, pp. 9–10.
12. *Ibid.*, pp. 6 ff.
13. *Ibid.*, pp. 7 ff.

Thracians, while Odysseus drags the dying men aside to give free egress for the horses, "that they might not fear when they trod upon the dead, for they were not yet accustomed to dead men." The king was slain in the midst of troubled sleep, the thirteenth victim.

The two Greeks recovered the spoils of Dolon, which Odysseus had placed on a tamarisk bush, and drove back with the white horses and gold chariot of the Thracian king to the Greek ships. Greeted joyously by Nestor Odysseus with ringing laughter drove the horses across the fosse and the other Achaeans went with him rejoicing. Odysseus placed the blood-stained spoils of Dolon in the stern of his ship, in order that they might make ready a sacred offering to Athena. They washed off their sweat in the sea, bathed in polished bathtubs, oiled themselves, and sat down to eat and drink.

The book is no crude old lay, but a cynical and sophisticated poem. The heroes of the *Iliad* are neither perfect nor base, but rather, as Aristotle[14] demands for the character of the hero, "men like other men." The poet of the *Iliad* knows when his heroes perform shameful acts, transgressing *aidos*. He makes us feel the *hubris* of Agamemnon and the tragic irony of Patroclus'[15] cynical speech, just before his own death, to Kebriones, on whom he rushes like "a lion, plundering the folds, struck in the heart, whose own daring destroys him." Sarpedon is, like Hector, one of the poet's great and tragic heroes; some of the most exquisite lines in the *Iliad* are written about him. Yet Patroclus expresses the wish to mutilate his dead body.

The critics who in defense of the *Doloneia* point to the hateful deeds and speeches of the heroes in the *Iliad* fail utterly to distinguish between what the Homeric hero may do and what the poet himself feels. The spirit of the

14. *Poetics,* 1453a; *Rhet.,* 1386a, 2, 8.
15. These passages, *Il.,* XVI, 559, 745 ff., are adduced by Shewan, *op. cit.,* p. 155, in defense of the low "heroic ideal" of the *Doloneia.*

lay of Dolon is shameless, cynical, and entirely its own. The occasional decorative beauty of its poetic descriptions contrasts with the barbarity of its main theme—the slaughter of helpless, sleeping men. This, more than any peculiarities of its language, convinces me that the book is an addition to the *Iliad* and that it was not composed by the "Master of Tragedy," who conceived the characters of Achilles and Hector and in the close of his great poem had ruth and pity triumph.

The Rhesus

In the late fifth century Euripides, or some poet writing under the influence of Euripides, saw in the *Doloneia* a theme for tragedy and dramatized the murder of the Thracian king and his followers in the play called by his name, *Rhesus*. The ascription of the play to Euripides has long been disputed and certainty about its authorship seems unattainable. Yet the beauty and glow of the lyric passages, the romantic description of the young Thracian king, child of the Mountain Muse and the Thracian River, and the pathos of the play are so Euripidean that I should hesitate to deny his authorship. Also, Professor Murray notes as most characteristic of Euripides "the sudden flavour of bitterness, the cold wind that so suddenly takes the heart out of joyous war." All these things and the sorrow which the drama expresses for human suffering go far toward convincing me that no other dramatist could have written it.

The play takes its plot directly from the *Doloneia,* but is far from being a real dramatization of that "Achaean" lay. The dramatic sympathy is shifted to the Trojan side, Hector is in the foreground, and the play closes with the Muse's lament for the murdered Rhesus. We cannot triumph with the Greeks; we mourn with the Thracians and Trojans. Rhesus is not idealized. He is depicted as a barbarian, generous, a staunch ally, "a child of battle and of song,"[16]

16. Murray, *Rhesus,* p. XII.

with the fierce heart of a warrior and the lust for vengeance
that has not become extinct in our warring world. He
boasts loudly and grandly and makes barbarous threats
that when he lays hands on Odysseus he will kill him by
a living torture. On hearing from Hector how Odysseus had
once come, disguised as a beggar, to spy in Troy and had
killed the guards before he escaped, Rhesus says:[17]

> No brave man kills his enemy by stealth,
> But meets him face to face and deals his blow.
> This man, who lurks in darkness like a thief,
> I will seize and through his living body drive
> A stake, and thus impale him at the Gate,
> Where birds of prey shall feed upon his flesh.
> Thus should a thief and temple-robber die!

This is sheer barbarism, by the standards of the fifth century
at least, if not by those of the Iron Age. It is uttered by a
Thracian, of a tribe which had at Athens an ill fame for
cruelty. Look at the awful example of Thracian blood-lust
related by Thucydides,[18] and his comment: "For the Thracian race is among the most bloodthirsty of barbarians,
when its spirit is up." The writer of the *Rhesus* knows that
the words of the king are barbaric, and in character. He
does not idealize his heroes—idealization is not the way
of Euripides.

The end of the play is pure Euripidean in its scene of
mother love. I quote in part Professor Murray's beautiful
translation of the lament of the Muse:

> My son shall not be laid in any grave
> Of darkness; this much guerdon will I crave
> Of Death's eternal bride, the heavenly-born
> Maid of Demeter, Life of fruits and corn,
> To set this one soul free. She owes me yet,
> For Orpheus widowed, an abiding debt.
> To me he still must be—that know I well—
> As one in death, who sees not. Where I dwell,

17. *Rhesus*, 510 ff. My translation.
18. *Thuc.*, VII, 29.

He must not come, nor see his mother's face.
Alone forever, in a caverned place
Of silver-veinéd earth, hid from men's sight,
A Man yet Spirit he shall live in light.
As under far Pangaion Orpheus lies,
Priest of great light and worshipped of the wise.

Then the bitterness and beauty of her last words

O fleshly loves of sad mortality,
O bitter motherhood of these that die,
She that hath wisdom will endure her doom,
The days of emptiness, the fruitless womb,
Not love, not bear love's children to the tomb.

I have given the translation by Professor Murray because of its understanding and beauty. It expands the thought of the original. The scene ends. The guards say: "The dead man sleepeth in his mother's care" (Murray).

Then come a few lines in which Hector gives orders for attack on the Greek wall and ships, to which the guards respond, "Obey our King! Onward to arms, ourselves and our allies. Heaven, on our side, might give us victory."

The end is not laughter and rejoicing, bathing and feasting, as in the *Doloneia,* but tears, anguish, and foreboding. There is no pity in the *Doloneia.* The poet who wrote the *Rhesus* has made a drama of pity, and this seems to me a sufficient answer to the criticism that the *Rhesus* "fails to excite the moral interest which is essential to a great drama."[19] The poet who chose for his theme the anguish of the defeated side, the agony of the victims of a "heroic" exploit, and the sorrow of a mother for her son murdered in war, has thereby deliberately moralized his drama. In many respects the *Rhesus* is a counterpart of that play of Euripides, which by this age is felt most deeply of all his plays, that drama which is "a picture of the inner side of a great conquest,"[20] and for a long period of years was

19. A. E. Haigh, *Tragic Drama of the Greeks,* p. 285. Oxford, 1896.
20. Murray, *Euripides and His Age,* p. 134. London and New York, 1913. See also his preface to his translation of the play.

esteemed lightly and called "the least interesting of the extant Greek tragedies";[21] namely, the *Trojan Women,* that great drama of the defeated and of pity. The "moral interest" of the two plays is the same. It is expressed by the god Poseidon in famous lines[22]—which apply to every generation.

Professor Murray's translation is well known.

> How are ye blind,
> Ye treaders down of cities, ye that cast
> Temples to desolation and lay waste
> Tombs, the untrodden sanctuaries where lie
> The ancient dead; yourselves so soon to die!

21. Haigh, *op. cit.,* pp. 300 f.
22. Euripides, *Trojan Women,* 95–97.

IV

THE GENTLER VIRTUES IN THE *ODYSSEY*

PROBABLY all critics agree that the *Iliad* precedes the *Odyssey* in date, though there is no unanimity on the question whether one poet composed both epics. Differences which exist between the poems are either explained away or ascribed to the assumed fact that the poet of the *Iliad* wrote the *Odyssey* late in his life,[1] or to the poet's desire[2] to produce a work of art entirely different from the *Iliad*, while others maintain that these differences "prove to every one who weighs them without prejudice that the *Iliad* and the *Odyssey* cannot have been composed in the same generation of men."[3]

Whether or not both poems were composed by one man, it is evident from the difference in their plots and contents that in the *Odyssey* there is a change from the *Iliad* in social, political, and religious outlook. In this chapter I inquire how far this change involves ethical standards and whether *aidos* and *eleos* have the same importance in the later poem as in the earlier.

Since the *Iliad* is tragic and the *Odyssey* a "comedy of manners,"[4] or a novel, rather than a heroic legend, there are not the same occasions for tragic pity and fear in the fascinating tale of the adventures of Odysseus as in the story of Ilium, the City at War. It is known from the beginning of the *Iliad* that Achilles is doomed to an early death and that "the day shall come when sacred Troy shall perish and Priam and the people of Priam of the ashen spear." That the *Odyssey* is to have a happy ending and that Odys-

1. Stawell, *op. cit.*, p. 120; J. W. Mackail, *Essays on Greek Poetry*, p. 12. London, 1910. Longinus IX, 12–15.
2. Allen, *op. cit.*, p. 200.
3. Nilsson, *Homer and Mycenae*, p. 137.
4. Longinus, *loc. cit.* 15.

seus is to return at last to his home and wife and son is
also evident from the first. The end of the *Iliad* is filled
with sorrow and pity for Hector, who died for his own
land. At the end of the *Odyssey* there is another triumph
over his enemies for Odysseus and an act of vengeance performed by him. Aristotle[5] gives the following summary of
the latter part of the *Odyssey:* "Odysseus comes back after
his stormy sea-faring, makes himself known, falls on his
enemies and destroys them." "The pleasure here is not that
of tragedy."[6]

With the help of kindly sea nymphs and Athena Odysseus
is equal to all perils by land and sea, and we feel only
the thrill and excitement of his adventures, knowing that
he does not need our pity and that he will triumph in the
end.

Hera, the vengeful goddess, does not appear in the *Odyssey*
and Athena manifests herself in far more pleasing aspects
than those of the war goddess of the *Iliad*. As protector of
Odysseus and Telemachus she makes delightful and romantic
epiphanies to them, appearing as a sea captain, a kind old
man, a little girl carrying a pitcher, a lovely young shepherd,
a woman fair and tall skilled in beautiful weaving. Even
when her help is given for vengeance on the offending
suitors, it appears more justifiable than her blind hatred
of Troy. Odysseus is no longer the relentless enemy of the
Trojans—those battles are past and gone. He is a struggler
against all kinds of dangers and temptations—monsters
of the deep, the cannibal Cyclops, the witch Circe, the love
of Calypso, the Sirens; he descends into Hades, where he
meets his mother's shade and the shades of his comrades in
battle. But we have no fears for him. His wanderings and
struggles are destined to have a "happy ending."

The *Odyssey* has pictures of cities at peace, Ithaca,
Sparta, Phaeacia, in contrast to the *Iliad* with its city at

5. *Poetics*, 1455b.
6. *Ibid.*, 1453a.

war. Its tales of adventure are romantic and removed from the life of every day to a fairy sea or land, where anything may happen—where, however, the human element is normal and reflects the everyday life.[7] Calypso and Circe, Helen and Penelope weave at their looms and the Cyclops looks after his sheep which he loves, and makes his cheeses. The virtues of organized society have an opportunity for expression which is not offered in the *Iliad,* where the only duty required is to fight and die for one's cause, Greek or Trojan, according to Hector's famous line,[8] "The one good omen is to defend the fatherland."

The word *eunomia,* abiding by custom or law (the later word for law, *nomos,* does not appear in either epic), occurs once in the *Odyssey,* contrasted with *hubris,* insolence, violence.

The quality *hubris* is characteristic of the suitors, and the word appears often in the description of their group. Because of this characterization, since the suitors play so large a part in the plot of the poem, the word *hubris* occurs more often in the *Odyssey* than in the *Iliad,* whereas *aidos* is a less frequent word in the *Odyssey* and its meaning is somewhat weakened. The decline of the importance of *aidos* in later Greek ethics is noted by Gilbert Murray,[9] who says of it: "It has quite ceased to be the guiding force of men's moral life."

In a well-ordered society like those pictured in the *Odyssey* the decline begins. Social life in Ithaca has been temporarily disturbed by the absence of the king, whereas life in Sparta[10] resembles the city at peace which the fire god inlaid in silver and gold on the shield of Achilles. There is the wedding feast in the palace, the music and the song, and the dancers whirling through the hall.[11] The city of

7. W. J. Woodhouse, *Composition of Homer's Odyssey,* p. 19. Oxford, 1930.
8. *Il.,* XII, 243.
9. *Greek Epic*[3], p. 89.
10. *Od.,* IV, 1 ff.
11. Cf. *Il.,* XVIII, 490 ff.

the Phaeacians is a glorified reflection of a town on a Mediterranean Greek island, flourishing in the happy arts of peace.

The gentle virtues of hospitality and friendship appear in beautiful ways in the *Odyssey*. There is nothing like the tragic, passionate devotion of Achilles to Patroclus, but there is the homely sweetness of ordinary human relations. The word *xeinos,* which means stranger, guest-friend, guest, and rarely, in the Homeric language, host, occurs considerably over one hundred times in the *Odyssey,* and a little more than a dozen times in the *Iliad*. Naturally, the chief meaning in the *Iliad* is "guest-friend," a friend in another land. The most beautiful example of the social institution which this Greek word connotes is the "guest-friendship" deriving from their respective grandfathers, discovered on the battlefield by the Aetolian–Argive Diomede and the Lycian Glaucus. Because of this relationship between their ancestors, Bellerophon and Oineus, Diomede says, "therefore I am a guest-friend to you in mid-Argos and you to me in Lycia, whenever I go to your land." Instead of fighting they exchanged their suits of armor, Glaucus giving Diomede his gold armor worth one hundred oxen for Diomede's bronze armor worth but five.[12] This is the most chivalrous of all the encounters in the *Iliad*.

In the *Odyssey* the meanings of stranger and guest-friend predominate. The abstract word for the relation of guest-friendship ξεινοσύνη appears (the only extant instance of the word) in the account of the formation of this tie between Odysseus and Iphitus of Oechalia.[13] The two met in Messene, where they had gone on similar errands, Odysseus, a lad sent by his father and the council to get recompense for three hundred sheep and their shepherds which Messenian pirates had stolen, Iphitus seeking to recover twelve broodmares with their young mules. They made formal friendship.

12. *Ibid.,* VI, 119 ff.
13. *Od.,* XXI, 15 ff.

Iphitus gave Odysseus the great bow which he had inherited from his father, Eurytus; Odysseus gave Iphitus a sword and spear, "the foundation of a close friendship, but they never came to know one another at the table."[14] The table is mentioned just before (*v.* 28), in the comment on the wicked deed of Heracles, who slew Iphitus, a guest in his house, disregarding the table (of hospitality), which he had spread before him. The table is mentioned in an oath which occurs three times in the *Odyssey:*[15] "Witness Zeus and the table of welcome and the hearth."

Zeus in the *Odyssey* is the god who protects strangers and is the god of hospitality.[16] As such Menelaus in the *Iliad*[17] prays to him: "Zeus, Lord on High, grant me that I avenge myself on him who wronged me, noble Alexander. Quell him beneath my lance, that another man may fear in time to be to wrong a host who gives him welcome." The word for host, ξεινοδόκος, used in this passage occurs only here in the *Iliad* and appears five times in the *Odyssey,* contrasted with ξεῖνος, guest.

The scenes of welcome in the *Odyssey* are delightful depictions of friendliness. Telemachus[18] greets the sea captain Mentes (really Athena) who stands in the outer porch of the palace at Ithaca. "Hail, Stranger! You shall be welcomed among us and when you have tasted food, you shall tell what your needs are." When Telemachus[19] and Mentor (Athena) reach Pylos, they find the Pylians offering sacrifice to Poseidon on the shore. Nestor's son placed a gold cup of sweet wine in Mentor's hand and, after they had drunk and eaten, Nestor asked who they were and what their errand was, whether they came as traders or sea robbers. Next, Telemachus and Nestor's son, Peisistratus, reach

14. *Ibid.,* XXI, 35 f.
15. *Ibid.,* XIV, 158; XVII, 155; XX, 230.
16. *Ibid.,* VI, 207; XIV, 58; *Il.,* XIII, 624, 625.
17. *Ibid.,* III, 353 f.
18. *Od.,* I, 113 ff.
19. *Ibid.,* III, 4 ff.

Sparta[20] and find the palace of Menelaus full of guests and
the gaiety of a double wedding feast. They halt their
chariots in the palace gateway and wait while the squire of
Menelaus asks his lord what he is to do about them. He
receives the reply: "You were no fool in time past, Eteoneus,
but now you babble folly like a child. Surely we two have
eaten the bread of many a man before we reached our home
in Sparta, hoping that Zeus would end our sorrows at the
last. But loose the horses and bring the strangers in to
feast."

The whole Spartan scene, its picture of the lovely housewife Helen with her gold distaff and bright-hued wools,
her charming recognition of Telemachus, her entertaining
narrative and that of Menelaus, and the pleasant speeding
of the parting guest form a perfect tale of hospitality and
friendship. Then in the sixth book there is young Nausíkaa
taking Odysseus under her protection, "for all strangers and
those in need are from Zeus and a little gift is sweet." In
the seventh book Odysseus sits in the palace of Alcinous,
by the hearth in the ashes, until Echeneus tells the king
that it is not fitting that a suppliant sit thus. "Bid him arise
and seat him on a silver-inlaid chair and give him wine,
and let the housewife give him food." Alcinous obeyed and
had his butler pour out wine to Zeus, who attends on suppliants. When Odysseus finally comes to his home in Ithaca,
where his own palace is full of the insolent and reveling
suitors, hospitality is given him by the swineherd, who tells
him that it is not right to fail to welcome a stranger, for
all such come from Zeus.

So the virtue of hospitality shines throughout the *Odyssey*,
whether the unbidden guest drinks from a gold cup and
eats fine food set on a beautiful table in the hall of kings,
where water from a gold pitcher is poured over his hands
into a silver basin, or sits on brushwood covered with a
goatskin in the humble steading of the swineherd, drinks

20. *Ibid.*, IV, 15 ff.

from a wooden bowl, and eats pork served on the spit on which it was roasted.

Hospitality on a grand scale that welcomes every stranger is essentially a virtue of the Epic Age. In later time the hearth remains a sacred place of refuge for the suppliant, but Homeric hospitality could not be maintained in the day of smaller things.

Love for family and friends is another of the epic gentler virtues in the *Odyssey*. It is not so poignant and passionate as in the *Iliad*, in which the heart of the tragedy lies in the love of Hector and Andromache, Achilles and Patroclus, the love of Thetis for her son, and the love of Priam and Hecuba for theirs, the love of Glaucus for Sarpedon, and the sad references to those at home who will mourn the loss of the warrior, never to return to his parents and his bride. In the *Odyssey* love is less tragic and is not frustrated. The longing of Odysseus for his home and wife, when he is staying with his beautiful sea-nymph mistress on her hidden isle, that of Penelope and Telemachus for the return of Odysseus, the devotion of the servants, Eurycleia and Eumaeus, the joy of old Laertes, when, faint with happiness, he holds his son in his arms, Odysseus' meeting in Hades with his mother who has died from sorrow at his loss, the recognition of Odysseus by his old hound, are full of tenderness, but the bitter sense of the certainty of impending loss and ruin is not there. In the *Iliad* everyone is doomed; in the *Odyssey* all is destined to be well.

In the earlier poem some of the gods exhibit malignant qualities, especially Hera and Athena, Ares and Aphrodite. In the *Odyssey* Athena[21] is practically the only deity who exercises an active influence, and her part is to protect the life and fortunes of Odysseus and his family, a more pleasing rôle than her activities as war goddess in the *Iliad*.

In the *Odyssey*[22] there are definitely bad men and women,

21. Except for Poseidon's anger.
22. "A fine mirror of the life of man," Aristotle, *Rhet.*, 1406b, 13.

designated as such; the *Iliad,* with the exception of the
rabble-rouser Thersites, has no villains. Outside that realm
of fancy and folklore where Circe and the lawless Cyclopes,
and the cannibal Laestrygonian giants dwell, "where the
ways of night and day meet," the wicked men in the *Odyssey*
are the princes from Ithaca, Dulichium, Same, and Zancyn-
thus, 108 in all, besides various serving men and a minstrel.[23]
Fifteen of these suitors are named in the poem. They
are mentioned as a group over 200 times and their conduct
is constantly described as insolent and wanton. The poet
makes some distinctions of character among them, Antinous
is uniformly brutal and insolent, Eurymachus is smooth-
spoken but hypocritical, Amphinomus is a misguided youth
with good impulses, but he shares the ruin of the other
suitors. Note also the protest made by some of the better-
minded suitors against the cruelty of Antinous in *Od.,* XVII,
481 ff.

The slaughter of the suitors, related in the twenty-second
book of the *Odyssey,* is unrelieved by any touch of humanity.
It is strange that anyone, contemplating that bloodied floor
strewn with corpses of men, who were not all guilty of
plotting the death of Telemachus, can feel satisfaction in
the murderous work. "The suitors," Bowra[24] says, "are
the victims of ἄτη, but they lack heroic or even loveable
qualities, and their death stirs not our pity, but our sense
of justice." But it is our horror, not our sense of justice,
that is stirred. At the end of the *Iliad* Achilles, softened
and pitiful, is a great human figure. At the end of the
Odyssey three good men, Odysseus, Telemachus, and Eumaeus are murderers taking delight in bloodshed and mutilation. Not even the seer Leiodes is spared. The torture and
mutilation of the goatherd Melanthius by Telemachus and
Eumaeus cannot be outdone by any obscenities of savagery
and is universally condemned, though often condoned. The

23. See Woodhouse, *op. cit.,* pp. 187–193.
24. Bowra, *op. cit.,* p. 26.

twelve maidservants who "slept with the suitors perforce" had to carry out the corpses of their lovers and cleanse their blood from the floor, chairs, and tables. When they had made the house decent, Telemachus had a horrible thought. The girls were driven into a narrow space outside the hall. Telemachus fastened a great rope high up on the wall of the room and put nooses, hanging from the rope, about the necks of the girls. By a single pull of the rope he strangled them all, their heads in a row, "that they might die most pitiably." He then proceeded to the horrid mutilation of Melanthius. What of our "sense of justice" here? This has been called[25] a work of savagery with which nothing else in Homer can be compared. The deed is whitewashed by various writers,[26] who fail to miss any condemnation by the poet of the vile acts.

Tears are shed and pity felt in the ending of the *Odyssey,* but for the "wrong side" dramatically. The father of Antinous shed tears for his son[27] and "pity seized all the Achaeans" at the sight. A special boon of strength is granted by Athena to the old Laertes, who, in the fighting that ensued after the slaughter of the suitors, killed the father who had wept for his son. Eupeithes fell, struck by Laertes' spear, and Odysseus and Telemachus attacked his supporters. They would have slain them all had not Athena checked them and made a covenant of peace between Odysseus and those who fought on the side of the kin of the suitors. It is a "happy ending," with nothing of the tragic grandeur of the close of the *Iliad.* It lacks ruth and pity.

There are many exquisitely pathetic scenes in the *Odyssey* which show the beautiful and gentle aspects of human nature—the meeting of Odysseus with his mother in the world of shadows, with his old father on the hillside; the old hound lying neglected in the filth of the farmyard,

25. Shewan, *op. cit.,* p. 156.
26. Woodhouse, *op. cit.,* pp. 192–193.
27. *Od.,* XXIV, 422 ff.

pricking up his ears at the sound of Odysseus' voice; then, as Odysseus came near him he moved his tail and dropped his ears, without strength to approach his master. "And the fate of black death took Argus when he had looked upon Odysseus again after twenty years."

The *Odyssey* is an absorbing tale of surpassing beauty, and a precious document revealing what gave pleasure to the people of the Iron Age. It is still, perhaps, the most delightful story ever written. But with all its beauty and its virtues of friendliness, hospitality, and family devotion, there is a savagery, reminiscent of folklore or saga, which comes out in the episodes which I have discussed. Woodhouse[28] attributes these to the tradition of the saga, "which does not mean that they are not Homer's work, every word of them." Gilbert Murray says, "the *Odyssey* is less rigorously cleaned up than the *Iliad*."[29]

Is there a touch of pity in the simile in which the dying girls are compared to birds? "As when thrushes on long wings or wood-doves fly to their nests and strike upon a net that is set in a thicket, where a deadly nesting awaits them."

Gilbert Murray[30] thinks that verse 473—"they struggled for a little while, but not for long"—is a "saving verse," inserted by a later poet. He adds, "the torture of women was unpleasant even to an audience which approved the cruelty to the goatherd."

Without attempting to decide the question of authorship by the part that ruth and pity have in the respective poems I argue that it is because of its profound humanity that the *Iliad* is a tragedy and a great moral story,[31] whereas in the *Odyssey*, for the most part devoid of deep tragic feeling, the civilized virtues of hospitality, kindness, and family affection have a wider scope because of the plot of the poem. The

28. Woodhouse, *op. cit.*, pp. 184 f.
29. Murray, *Greek Epic*[3], p. 127.
30. *Ibid.*
31. Bowra, *op. cit.*, p. 26.

Odyssey is a civilized poem, and the question asked in it about unknown peoples is significant of its standards. "Are they violent and savage and lawless, or are they kind to strangers and have they god-fearing hearts?"[32]

32. *Od.*, VI, 121; VIII, 576; IX, 176; XIII, 202. Hoffman, *op. cit.*, pp. 101 f., notes that ethical terminology plays a greater part in the *Odyssey* than in the *Iliad*. He remarks that social consciousness had developed further in the later poem, creating new terms that were not at the command of the poet of the *Iliad*.

V

HUMANITY IN HESIOD

"Hesiod who often summons us to righteousness and thrift."
(Plutarch)[1]

HESIOD'S poetry, following immediately after the Homeric epic, has been so dwarfed by comparison with the *Iliad* and *Odyssey* that its peculiar value and merits have not been fully realized until a recent period. Now scholars call Hesiod "the first in the line of great thinkers that Europe has produced,"[2] "the first religious thinker in Europe,"[3] "the first preacher of labor and of the rights of the poor."[4]

From his poems, *Works and Days* and the *Theogony,* we learn of the living conditions, the government, and ethical and religious beliefs of the peasants of Boeotia in the period which is known as the Dark Age of Greece. He lived in the eighth century[5] B.C., probably a generation or two after the composer of the *Odyssey.* He himself calls the age in which he lived, as we still call it, the Iron Age.

He uses the outward patterns of composition which he inherited from the poets of the heroic epic, the hexameter verse, the epic phrases, and the Ionic language, but his themes and spirit are far removed from the stories of heroic battles and heroic adventure. In the introduction to his poem, *Works and Days,* he says that he wishes to tell of realities and he is the first European author to deal with problems of labor and the relations between the "Haves" and the "Have-nots" in human society. The remark[6] of

1. *Comparison of Aristides and Cato,* III.
2. E. Meyer, *Kleine Schriften,* II, 17 ff. Halle, 1924.
Hesiod's Erga und das Gedicht von den fünf Menschengeschlechtern.
3. F. M. Cornford, *From Religion to Philosophy,* p. 5. New York, 1912.
O. Kern, *Die Religion der Griechen,* I, 258. Berlin, 1926.
4. E. Schwartz, *Charakterköpfe aus der antiken Literatur,* I, 9. Leipzig, 1906.
5. Allen, *Homer, Origins and Transmissions,* pp. 89 ff.
6. Plut., *Moralia,* 223 A.

Cleomenes of Sparta that Homer was "the poet of the Spartans, and Hesiod of the Helots, for Homer had given the rules for fighting and Hesiod for farming," indicates a reason for Hesiod's fame and value as a source for social life in early Greece.

Works and Days is a guide for the farmer and small trader and a calendar of lucky and unlucky days—"some a mother and some a stepmother." It is also a moral treatise and its theme is social justice. The word *dike,* justice, occurs often in the poem—to be exact, twenty-four times.[7] Hesiod is the first of the extant Greek poets to exalt this virtue, and to personify Justice as a goddess, daughter of Zeus and Themis, and sharer of Zeus's throne. The word *dike* appears in the *Iliad* four times in the singular and once in the plural, in the *Odyssey* eight times in the singular and three times in the plural. In the *Odyssey* it is most frequently used in the phrase, "as is the *custom*" of kings, mortals, old men, etc. Sometimes in the *Iliad* and *Odyssey* the word means justice, as in *Od.* XIV, 84. "The Gods honor justice and good deeds." In the same meaning and in an absolutely Hesiodic passage δίκη appears in *Il.*, XVI, 387–388. "When Zeus is angry with men when they judge the laws crookedly in the assembly, and drive out justice, disregarding the vengeance of the gods" (cf. *Works and Days,* 262).

In *Work and Days* the word *aidos* is seldom used, but it appears in a very famous personification, coupled with *Nemesis.*[8] In Hesiod's other long poem, the *Theogony,* the word *dike* occurs in a list of personified moral qualities, daughters of Zeus and Themis.[9]

Hesiod's theme is indicated in *Works and Days,* lines 2 ff., in words which call to mind the language of the Psalms and of the poet Aeschylus.

"For Zeus easily gives strength and easily brings down

7. It often means *judgment, decision of the judge.*
8. *W. and D.,* 195–201.
9. *Th.,* 902.

the strong; he easily humbles the mighty and exalts him who is of low degree; easily he makes straight the crooked and destroys the haughty man—Zeus, the Lord of Thunder, who dwells on high. Behold and hear and make judgments straight by means of justice."[10] His dispute with his brother about their inheritance and the rights of that case are here referred to, but "justice" is soon generalized and personified in the "virgin Justice,"[11] who sits beside her father Zeus and tells him of the wickedness of men, when justice is transgressed. Again, "When[12] Justice is mishandled and haled away by the bribe-takers who decide the laws with crooked judgment, there is tumult and outcry. Shedding tears, she follows through the city and the haunts of men, clothed in mist, bringing evil to those who drove her out, who give unrighteous judgment."

The myths and the fable with which Hesiod enforces his teaching are famous and have had a great influence on European literature. They are, the *Theft of Fire by Prometheus*,[13] and the consequent anger of Zeus against man, who had received the fire; the making of the *Greek Eve, Pandora*, fashioned by the Fire God at the bidding of Zeus, to be a curse to men—a thing of beauty, but full of lies; the *Fall of Man*[14] that came with the woman and her jar of pests; the *Five Ages of Man*, Gold, Silver, Bronze, Heroic, and Iron; and the fable for princes, the *Hawk and the Nightingale*.

A comparison is inevitable between the myths in *Works and Days* and those in Genesis in the Old Testament, which

10. *W. and D.*, 6 ff.
11. *Ibid.*, 256 ff.
12. *Ibid.*, 220 ff.
13. *The Prometheus Bound* of Aeschylus is the only extant Greek tragedy taken from Hesiod's *Theogony*, where the myth of Prometheus appears in longer form.
14. Cf. Meyer, *op. cit.*, pp. 36, 37. (The Golden Age the time before Prometheus stole fire and Pandora opened her jar of pests for mankind.)

have a long history behind them.[15] The resemblance is so striking that older scholars have been convinced that they cannot be accidental.[16] Reitzenstein[17] has recently argued that oriental (Persian) ideas may have influenced Hesiod, since his father was born in Aeolian Cyme in Asia Minor and immigrated into Boeotia. He says that we must reckon with a great mutual exchange of ideas among the various religions in Asia Minor in the early Hellenic period.[18] And it seems inevitable that Hesiod should have learned much from his Asiatic[19] father.

The possibility that various Babylonian and Persian myths are reflected by way of Ionia in Hesiod is most interesting and likely, but not yet proved. The evident spiritual likeness between Hesiod and the Hebrew prophets of the eighth century may often be satisfactorily explained by the similar conditions in which Hesiod and Hosea, Amos and Micah wrote.[20] The poverty of the people and the oppression of the princes roused two contemporary shepherds of genius, Hesiod in Boeotian Ascra and Amos in Judaea to protest in flaming words against unjust rulers. Hesiod's morality is similar to that of Amos[21] and Micah in its bitter hatred of sin and the sinner. His condemnations of evil are in many respects like those of the Ten Commandments. He denounces theft, adultery, mistreatment of parents, false witness, and greed. He adds to his list of wicked deeds sins against orphans and wrong done to a suppliant or guest. Zeus is said by him to have thirty thousand spirits, clothed

15. Cf. J. A. Bewer, *The Literature of the Old Testament*, pp. 60 f. New York, 1924.

16. F. A. Paley, *The Epics of Hesiod*, pp. 20, 21. London, 1883.

17. R. Reitzenstein, *Warburg Bibliothek*, VII, 38 ff., 58, 65 f. 1926. *Von Töpferorakel zu Hesiod.*

18. *Ibid.*, pp. 65 f.

19. *W. and D.*, 635 ff.

20. Kern, *op. cit.*, I, 266, 297.

Meyer, *op. cit.*, pp. 24 ff.

Schwartz, *op. cit.*, pp. 6, 8 f.

21. Cf. Amos 2. 6, "because they sold the righteous for silver and the poor for a pair of shoes," with Hesiod, *W. and D.*, 262 ff. *et pass.*

in mist, who roam up and down the earth, watching judgments and evil deeds.[22]

Hesiod and Amos,[23] living in bad times, look to their god,
Zeus or Jehovah, to punish wickedness and oppression and
to reward the righteous man. The language of the prophets
is grander, their denunciations more fiery, and the threats
of Jehovah more bloodcurdling than the utterances in the
similar passages in Hesiod, but there is often an astonishing
resemblance in statement or prophecy.

In *Works and Days,* 180 ff., Hesiod prophesies that Zeus
shall destroy the race of Iron Age men when they are born
with gray hairs on their temples[24] (i.e., are physically degen-
erate).[25]

The father shall be at feud with his child and the child with
his father, the guest with his host and comrade with comrade.
Brother shall not love brother as before. Men shall dishonour
their aging parents and shall assail them with bitter words, cruel-
hearted, and having no regard for the gods. They shall not repay
to their old parents the cost of rearing them and one man shall
sack another's city. There shall be no pleasure in the man who
keeps his oath nor in the honest man, nor in the good, but men
shall praise the doer of evil and his violence. Strength of fist shall
settle right and sense of shame shall disappear. The bad man
shall injure the better, attacking him with crooked speech and
swearing a false oath. Jealousy, with ugly words, rejoicing in
iniquity, and with hateful face, shall haunt all men. And then
at last Aidos and Nemesis [ruth and retribution] wrapping their
loveliness in white garments shall leave the wide-wayed earth,
abandoning mankind, and shall go to Olympus, and the company
of the Immortals. And bitter griefs shall be left for mortal men
and there shall be no defense against evil.

22. Reitzenstein, *op. cit.,* p. 63; cf. R. H. Charles, *The Book of Jubilees* (London, 1902), pp. 33 f. "the angels of the Lord descended on the earth, those who
are named the Watchers, that they should instruct the children of men and
that they should do judgment and uprightness on the earth."

23. Wilamowitz-Moellendorff, *Antigonos von Karystos* (Berlin, 1881), p.
314, "dem hirten von Thekoa tritt der hirt von Askra nicht unebenbürtig
gegenüber."

24. Cf. Reitzenstein, *op. cit.,* pp. 55, 63.

25. *W. and D.,* 180 ff.

The passage about *Aidos* and *Nemesis* is very famous and is copied by Virgil in *Georgics*, II, 473 f.

> *extrema per illos*
> *Justitia excedens terris vestigia fecit*

And in *Eclogues*, IV, 6

> *Iam redit et Virgo.*

Ovid also has it in *Met.*, I, 150.

> *ultima caelestum terras Astraea reliquit.*

In *Il.*, XIII, 122, the two words are coupled, but neither is ever personified in Homer. To the lines that prophesy the destruction of all ties of fidelity and the dying out of all decencies there is a striking parallel in Micah (7.2 ff.)[26]

The good man is perished out of the earth; and there is none upright among men. They all lie in wait for blood; they hunt every man his brother with a net. Their hands are upon that which is evil to do it diligently; the prince asketh and the judge is ready for a reward; and the great man he uttereth the mischief of his soul—Trust ye not in a friend, put not your confidence in a guide; keep the doors of your mouth from her that lieth in thy bosom. For the son dishonoreth the father, the daughter riseth up against her mother, the daughter-in-law against her mother-in-law; a man's enemies are those of his own house.

Mackail[27] has noted that when Hesiod rises into the epic tone, his language is like that of the Hebrew prophets who were the first voice of democracy. Many coincidences of thought could be adduced. I will give but one more, that between *Works and Days*, 225 ff. and the fourth chapter of Micah and the eleventh chapter of Isaiah. In each a picture is given of the happiness that attends the righteous.

---

26. For discussions of the date of this passage see *The International Critical Commentary*, Smith, Ward and Bewer, *Micah*, etc., pp. 138 f. New York, 1911; G. B. Gray, *Critical Introduction to the Old Testament*, pp. 219 f. New York, 1913.

27. *Lectures on Greek Poetry*, pp. 30 f. London, 1915.

Hesiod.[28] But they that give straight judgment to strangers and to the people and walk in the path of justice, their city blooms and the people prosper in it. Peace, nurse of children, abides in the land and far-seeing Zeus never ordains bitter war against them. Neither hunger nor disaster ever dwell with men of righteous judgment, but they till with joy the fields which they love. The earth bears for them abundant food, the oak on the hills bears acorns at the top, in its midst the bee. Their fleecy sheep are heavy with wool. Their wives bear children like their fathers. They flourish forever with good things and do not fare on ships, for the wheat-bearing earth gives them its crop.

Micah 4. 1–4 = Isaiah 2. 2–4.[29] For out of Zion shall go forth the law and the word of the Lord from Jerusalem, and he shall judge between many peoples and shall reprove strong nations afar off; and they shall beat their swords into plow-shares and their spears into pruning hooks; nation shall not lift up sword against nation, neither shall they learn war any more. But they shall sit every man under his vine and under his fig-tree; and none shall make them afraid; for the mouth of the Lord of Hosts hath spoken it.

Isaiah 11. 1–9.[30] And righteousness shall be the girdle of his loins, and faithfulness the girdle of his reins. The wolf also shall dwell with the lamb and the leopard shall lie down with the kid; and the calf, and the young lion and the fatling together; and a little child shall lead them. And the cow and the bear shall feed; their young ones shall lie down together and the lion shall eat straw like the ox. And the sucking child shall place his hand on the cockatrice' den. They shall not hurt nor destroy in all my holy mountain; for the earth shall be full of the knowledge of the Lord, as the waters cover the sea.

---

28. *W. and D.*, 224 ff.

29. For later dating of these two passages see G. W. Wade, *The Book of Isaiah (Westminster Commentaries)*, p. 14, London, 1911; R. E. Wolfe, *Zeitschrift für die alttestamentliche Wissenschaft und die Kunde des nachbiblischen Judentums*, XII, 93–94, Berlin, 1935, *The Late Exilic Editor;* Smith, Ward and Bewer, *op. cit.*, pp. 82–84.

30. For the dating of Isaiah 11. 1–9 see Wolfe, *op. cit.*, pp. 98–99, *The Messianist* (519–445 2.3.); Wade, *op. cit.*, pp. 81 f. (eighth century), and Bewer, *The Literature of the Old Testament*, pp. 114 ff., New York, 1924 (eighth century).

These descriptions of a happy age have had many echoes, the most celebrated of which are the much-discussed fourth *Eclogue* of Virgil and Horace's sixteenth *Epode*.

Many other passages could be quoted to show the close analogy between Hesiod and the prophets of the Old Testament.[31]

In the early part of *Works and Days, dike,* justice, is a recurring word. Near the end of this section of the poem (276 ff.) there is a distinction made between man and beast as follows:

For the son of Cronos established this law for mankind, that fishes and beasts and winged birds should devour one another since justice is not in them, but to mankind he gave justice, which proves the best by far. For whoever knows what is just and is willing to speak it, far-seeing Zeus gives him good fortune, but if a man voluntarily lies in his witness and swears a false oath, and hurts justice, and sins beyond repair, that man's generation is left in darkness, but the generation of an oath-keeping man is ever better thereafter.

This and later passages in *Works and Days,* where honesty is commended as the best policy, are said by J. A. Symonds[32] to reveal "the spirit of a prudent clown, the practical and calculating selfishness which the doleful conditions of the early age of Hellenic civilization intensified." In support of this criticism of Hesiod's ethical teaching, he quotes, out of its context, and mistranslates, as follows, line 686 of *Works and Days,* "Money is a man's soul"; whereas Hesiod, telling of the risks taken by the Greek tradesman at sea, says, "in their ignorance men venture it (i.e. the dangerous spring sailing), for *their gains mean life to poor mortals,* but it is dreadful to die in the waves."

31. Schwartz, *op. cit.,* pp. 6–8. Meyer, *op. cit.,* p. 29 n. 2. "Es gibt psychologisch kaum ein interessanteres und lehrenreicheres Studium als die richtige Interpretation Hesiods; die nächste Analogie bieten auch hier die alttestamentlichen Propheten."
32. *Studies of the Greek Poets,* I, 164. London, 1893.

There is an identity of thought between Hesiod's promise of prosperity to the righteous and that of the Psalmist.[33] "Trust in the Lord and do good; so shall thou dwell in the land and verily thou shall be fed." "Depart from evil and do good, and dwell forever more." "For the Lord loveth judgment and forsaketh not his saints; they are preserved forever, but the seed of the wicked shall be cut off." "The righteous shall inherit the land and dwell therein forever." If these verses were put into Hesiodic hexameter and the name of Zeus substituted for that of the Lord, they would be absolutely appropriate to the tenor of the moralizing part of *Works and Days*.

The ἀγάπη, love, theme of Paul's wonderful chapter in his first epistle to the Corinthians "rejoices not in injustice." This eulogy of the highest virtue that the thought and acts of men have achieved is foreshadowed by Hesiod's simple eulogy of justice, that distinguishes man from beast.

Hesiod's other poem, the *Theogony*, is not concerned with moral questions, but with the coming into existence of gods and their offspring, after the primeval beings, Chaos, Earth, and the reproductive principle, Eros, have arisen and brought forth various children. It tells of old gods, still in Hesiod's time worshiped in the countryside, and of the new gods of Olympus, Zeus and his retinue, the "Mycenaean"[34] gods of the Heroic Age. Its crude and primitive stories about the gods, especially the macabre description of the mutilation of Heaven (Uranus) by his son Cronos, and of the deities that sprang from the drops of his blood fertilizing Earth, have no ethical value, but preserve the rude imaginings of poets of an earlier period. They are called "ugly tales" by Plato.[35]

The *Theogony* has many lists of personified abstractions, which sometimes appear later as mythological persons—Har-

33. Psalm 37. 3, 27 ff. *Et pass.* in the Psalms.
34. Nilsson, *op. cit.*, p. 267.
35. Plato, *Republic*, pp. 377–378.

monia, Eurynome, the three Graces, Aglaia, Euphrosyne, Thalia, Mnemosyne, Eirene, Metis. As Kern[36] says, it is difficult to estimate to what extent the simple peasant of Ascra has influenced the worship of personifications, in the course of centuries. In them Kern finds Hesiod's true religious convictions.

There can be no doubt that the moral abstraction that most deeply influenced his thought was justice and this he handed on to Aeschylus, who writes of justice more grandly, but with no deeper moral conviction than Hesiod.[37] The justice that Hesiod demands for the humble laborer of his Dark Age, oppressed by the ruling class, is the theme of a chorus of the Agamemnon.[38] "But Justice gleams bright in a smoke-stained hut. She honors the righteous man, but from the palace decked with gold, where hands are black with guilt, she turns away with eyes aloof, and goes to pious homes, rejecting the power of wealth mis-stamped with praise. She brings all things to their goal."

I have elsewhere[39] traced the evolution of Wordsworth's *Ode to Duty* back to Aeschylus, through the intermediate poems of Gray (his *Hymn* or *Ode to Adversity*), Horace (*Ode to Fortune,* I., 35), and the Reverend James Merrick's[40] translation of Mesomedes' *Ode to Nemesis,*[41] which, though a slight thing, has reminiscences of Aeschylus, whose Justice derives from Hesiod.

The "homely poet of Rydal"[42] had a vision of nature and an ethical code to which the homely poet of Ascra could not attain, but Hesiod's praise of Justice flowered after many centuries in Wordsworth's *Ode to Duty,* "Stern daughter of the Voice of God," Hesiod's παρθένος Διός.

36. *Op. cit.,* I, 257.
37. Cf. Aeschylus, *Sept.,* 662, with Hesiod, *W. and D.,* 256.
38. Aeschylus, *Ag.,* 773 ff.
39. *Classical Weekly,* IV (1910), 58 ff. "The Classical Element in Gray's Poetry."
40. A contemporary of Gray, not mentioned by him.
41. F. Bellermann, *Die Hymnen des Dionysius und Mesomedes.* Berlin, 1840.
42. Matthew Arnold's phrase.

Stern Law giver! yet thou dost wear
The Godhead's most benignant grace.
Nor know we anything so fair
As in the smile upon Thy face.
Flowers laugh before Thee on their beds
And fragrance in Thy footing treads.
Thou dost preserve the Stars from wrong,
And the most ancient Heavens, through
    Thee, are fresh and strong.

VI

PERSONIFIED VIRTUES

H OMER has few personifications, but several of them never disappear from the Greek literature. The most famous are Moira, Destiny, a power to which gods[1] and men are subject, Ate, the spirit of Mischief, the "eldest daughter of Zeus, who brings all men to folly,"[2] and Themis, the goddess of established custom and right.[3] These are all personifications of common nouns, *moira,* portion, allotment, *ate,* folly, ruin, and *themis,* right—very frequent words in the Homeric vocabulary. Moira[4] is moralized in Homer, a "projection of the social structure," and in one place in the *Iliad*[5] is in the plural, as it is in the *Theogony*[6] of Hesiod, where the names Klotho, Spinner, Lachesis, Allotter, and Atropos, the Inflexible, are given. Themis in the *Iliad* has for her function, as her name indicates, established order and organization. She summons and dismisses assemblies and looks after the order of precedence on Olympus (in *Il.,* XV, 95, the ordering of the banquet of the gods). She appears as a personified divinity three times in the *Iliad*[7] and once in the *Odyssey.*[8] Ate[9] has a more particular descrip-

1. *Il.,* XVI, 431 ff.
2. *Ibid.,* IX, 505; XIX, 91, 126, 129, 137 ff.
3. *Ibid.,* XV, 87 ff., XX, 4; *Od.,* II, 68.
4. Cornford, *From Religion to Philosophy,* p. 51. "Moira came to be supreme in Nature over all the subordinate wills of men and Gods, because she was first supreme in human society, which was continuous with Nature." *Op. cit.,* chaps. I, II.
   J. L. Myres, *Political Ideas of the Greeks,* p. 183. New York, 1927.
5. *Il.,* XXIV, 49; in *Od.,* VII, 197, the Moirae are called *Klothes, Spinners.*
6. *Theogony,* 216 f., 904 f.
7. *Il.,* XV, 87 ff., XX, 4; *Od.,* II, 68 f.
8. The phrase ἦ θέμις ἐστί, "as is right," *"comme il faut,"* is usual in both the *Iliad* and the *Odyssey.* In the *Odyssey* δίκη appears in a similar phrase. It is probable that from these recurring phrases the idea of a goddess Themis and a goddess Dike (*Theog.,* 901 f.) was evolved.
9. *Il.,* IX, 505; XIX, 92 ff., 126, 129, 137 f.

tion than either of the other two. She is strong and swift-
footed and outruns the Prayers of Penitence, who are also
daughters of Zeus. She walks with delicate feet above the
heads of men and does them harm. Because of her help to
Hera against the infant Heracles, son of Zeus, Zeus hurled
her from Heaven, never to return. Ate, Themis, and Moira
all appear in tragedy,[10] and Moira and Themis in the philosophers. The descriptions of Ate in Homer are fanciful and in-
consistent. In Hesiod she is a comrade of Lawlessness, in
Theogony, 230; in *Works and Days* the word is not personified, and in three times out of the four cases is plural.[11] The
common noun is always far more usual than the personification, and in Sophocles, where the word is frequent, it appears
never to be personified. Aeschylus, rich in personification,
has Ate for one of his terrible goddesses. Clytemnestra swears
an oath by "the Dike fulfilled of her daughter" Iphigenia, by
Ate and Erinys, that "her hope does not tread in halls of
fear," while Aegisthus kindles the flame upon her hearth.
The word is tragic and does not appear in comedy or in Attic prose.[12]

Hesiod is the first great personifier. In his *Theogony* various personified abstract qualities which are attributed to
Zeus are said to be his wives or daughters. Among his wives
are Metis, Wisdom (mother of Athena), Themis, and Mnemosyne, Memory, mother of the Muses; among his daughters is the triad Eunomia, Dike, and Eirene, Order, Justice,
Peace. This triad remains constant in the time of the Lawgivers and later. Aidōs, Mercy, sits beside Zeus as *paredros*,
in the *Oedipus at Colonus* of Sophocles.[13] In that play Polynices, hoping to win his father's forgiveness and so get his

---

10. Cf. Shakespeare, *Julius Caesar*, III, 1, 63.
        "And Caesar's spirit, ranging for revenge,
            With Ate at his side, come hot from hell."
Cf. *Much Ado*, "the infernal Ate," cf. Aesch., *Ag.*, 1433.
11. *Love's Labour's Lost*, IV, 2, 67, "More Ates! More Ates!"
12. Liddell and Scott, new edition, *s.v.*
13. Sophocles, *O. C.*, 1267 f.

aid against his brother Eteocles, says: "Mercy shares the throne of Zeus, in all his acts." His words recall a famous passage.

> It is enthronèd in the hearts of kings,
> It is an attribute of God himself;
> And earthly power doth then show likest God's
> When mercy seasons justice.[14]

It is not known how early the altars to Mercy and to Pity mentioned by Pausanias[15] were established. He says of the Altar of Pity that Pity is the god most helpful in human life and changes of fortune and that the Athenians are the only Greeks who give honors to Pity. "Not only is philanthropy established among them, but also they show more piety to the gods than the rest of the world."

The most famous reference to this altar is in Lucian's life of Demonax.[16] When the Athenians, to rival Corinth, were discussing the proposition to establish gladiatorial contests in Athens, Demonax came forward in the assembly and said, "Do not vote for this, Athenians, until you overthrow the Altar to Pity." A famous description of the altar and its suppliants was written by Statius.[17] The Latin poet calls it the altar of gentle Clemency—"mitis posuit Clementia sedem."

The goddess listens to prayers night and day. There is but little of superstitious rite, no incense, no bloodshed on the altar; locks of hair and garments are hung about it. There is no image of the deity. She does not appear in bronze or gold or silver, but delights to dwell in the heart and mind. This passage in Statius is reminiscent of a sentence in pseudo-Demosthenes,[18] which says that whereas all men have altars of Justice, Order, and Mercy, the most beautiful and holy are in each man's soul and nature.

14. Shakespeare, *Merchant of Venice*, IV, 1, 193.
15. Paus., I, 17, 1.
16. Lucian, *Demonax*, 57 (a Cynic philosopher of the second century after Christ).
17. Stat., *Theb.*, XII, 481–505.
18. [Dem.] XXV, 35.

The altar to Pity in Athens is first mentioned by Apollodorus[19] and is frequently referred to in later writers. An inscription found in the sanctuary at Epidaurus records that Hierocles dedicated an altar to Pity there in obedience to a dream.[20]

It is natural to find the goddess Eunomia in a fragment of Alcman[21] and as the title of a poem by Tyrtaeus, since both of these poets worked in Sparta, a state that loved organization; it is equally appropriate to find Eunomia personified in a poem by Solon,[22] the Athenian Lawgiver. Alcman calls Fortune "sister of Order and Persuasion and daughter of Forethought." The genealogy of Fortune in Alcman's fragment is not consistent with that in Hesiod.[23] With an abundance of ethical abstracts at their command the poets deal freely with them, following Hesiod's example in deifying a quality at will. These new deities are often inventions to suit the hour and have no cult,[24] while others, like Mercy and Pity, answer to some strong human need and have a continuing worship.

The moralization of Zeus after the heroic period, in which he is a projection of the Mycenaean kingship,[25] is indicated by virtues assigned to him as sharers of his throne or as wives and daughters. There is no case of this in Homer. In the poetry of the eighteenth century such attributes share the throne of kings, as in Collins' *Ode to Mercy;*

"Thou, thou shalt rule, our queen, and[26] share our monarch's throne."

19. Apollodorus, *Bibl.*, II, 8, 1; III, 7, 1.
20. I. G., IV, 1282, 91.
21. Diehl, *Anthologia Lyrica*, Alcman, 44.
Cf. Bowra, *Greek Lyric Poetry*, p. 67. Oxford, 1936.
22. Diehl, *Solo*, 3, 32. This is not necessarily personification.
23. Cf. *Theogony*, 349, 366.
24. Eunomia had a shrine on Akro-Corinth.
25. Nilsson, *Homer and Mycenae*, pp. 269 ff.
26. Cf. also Collins' *Ode to Peace*, and his *Ode to Liberty—*
    "Thou, lady—thou shalt rule the west!"

It was inevitable as the kingship in Greece disappeared or was diminished in power that the Greek imagination, always fertile in producing new deities from epithets of the old gods, should personify and deify more and more abstractions which express the political, philosophical, and religious ideas of the age of the Lawgivers and early philosophers. Themis is a goddess in Homer, Dike in Hesiod[27]; and these continue to be honored together with Eunomia (merely the name of the concept in the *Odyssey*) and Nomos (not found in Homer), which assumes the new meaning of Law in place of the older one of *Custom*. These two abstractions naturally become personified and take their place among the deified or semideified abstractions of the new political and philosophical writers and thinkers. Ananke, Necessity, appears among the philosophers[28] as an important abstract deity. "These powers are written with capital letters and are called gods, but they are without personality and individuality because they are each nothing but a power of a certain kind." Nilsson[29] here speaks of the Homeric personifications of the spirits of evil and of war, but what he writes is true of most of the intellectual and civilized personifications as well.

The genealogies of these abstract qualities vary in the various poets. In Hesiod Themis is the mother of Dike.[30] The Orphic theogony makes Dike daughter of Nomos (Law) and Eusebeia (Piety).[31] In *Prometheus Bound*[32] Themis is Gaia (Earth), "one form of many names." In the *Choephori*[33] Gaia is mother of Themis, as she is in the *Theogony*. Solon[34] makes Koros, Satiety, the parent of Hubris, Insolence, in which he is followed by Theognis,[35] while Pindar reverses

27. Cf. Diehl, *Solo*, 3, 14.
28. Parmenides, *Frags.* 8, 30. Cf. Euripides, *Troades*, 887.
29. *Greek Religion*, p. 172. Oxford, 1925.
30. *Th.* 901 f.
31. Orph., *Frags.* 159, 160.
32. Aesch. *P. V.*, 211 f.
33. *Id. Cho.*, 2.
34. Diehl, *Solo*, I, 58.
35. Theognis, 153.

the relationship and calls Hubris the mother of Koros.[36]
Pindar follows Hesiod in giving the triad of daughters, Eunomia, Dike, and Eirene, to Themis as their mother. He says
of Corinth: "[37]For therein dwell Order and her sisters, sure
foundation of states, Justice and like-minded Peace, dis-
pensers of wealth to men, wise Themis' golden daughters."
Themis in Pindar,[38] like her daughter Dike in Hesiod, sits
beside Zeus; "Aigina of the long oars, where saviour Themis,
who sitteth in judgment by Zeus, the stranger's succour, is
honored more than elsewhere among men."[39]

Many of these personifications which belong to the early
age of Greek religious thought, such as the Muses, the Char-
ites (Graces), and the Erinyes (Avengers of blood), are as familiar and well known to the Greeks of all ages as the greater
gods themselves. Others have no individuality and are not
anthropomorphized at all, but remain abstractions.

Hesiod, who, as we have seen, was the great personifier of
abstract ideas, handed down to the lyric poets and the tragedians a wealth of ethical personifications. His Justice, under
its later name *dikaiosyne,* appears in a beautiful fragment of
Euripides, quoted by Aristotle.[40]

> The golden face of Justice—
> Not evening star nor morning star
> So marvelous as this.

36. Pindar, *Ol.,* XIII, 10.
37. Pindar, *op. cit.,* XIII, 7. Myers' translation.
38. *Op. cit.,* VIII, 22. Myers' translation.
39. Myres, *op. cit.,* "Themis Personified," pp. 135 ff. "The Notion of Justice," pp. 180 ff. In this fine discussion of Themis and Dike, Professor Myres
appears to have misunderstood *Il.,* XVI, 388; "disregarding the *vengeance* of
the gods" he translates "not regarding the voice of the gods," and hence he
considers Themis "the Voice of the Gods." Cf. *op. cit.,* pp. 131 f.
40. Nauck, *Eur.,* 486; *Tragicorum Graecorum Fragmenta,* Leipzig, 1889;
Aristotle, *Ethics,* 1129b, 28 (arranged by Meineke, from *The Wise Melanippe*).

VII

VIRTUE IN SOLON, THEOGNIS, SIMONIDES, PINDAR, AND BACCHYLIDES

THE virtue of justice continues to be celebrated by the sixth-century elegiac poets, Solon the famous Athenian Lawgiver, and Theognis the poet of Megara, who hates democracy, in whose eyes the "good" man is in general the aristocrat. In spite of his political fierceness, the result of the bitter party struggles in his country, Theognis utters some fine commendations of the virtues already established in the older literature. Among his notable verses are these, in which he honors good faith toward a guest and suppliant, piety, and justice.[1]

"No mortal who cheated a guest or a suppliant, son of Polypaus, ever escaped the eyes of the Immortals. Choose rather to dwell in poverty and piety than to be a rich man, who has gained wealth unjustly. In justice, in a word, is all virtue and, Cyrnus, all good men are just."

Solon, the political reformer in early sixth-century Athens, like Theognis, is not a great poet and writes in verse because prose had not yet been developed as a means of literary communication. His poetry informs us of the desperate social state of Athens in his time and of his reforms of the bad conditions in the case of debtors and in the economic inferiority of Athens. I have already noted his praise of Eunomia and here translate the entire passage.[2]

The Goddess of Law (Eunomia) brings all things into order and harmony and puts many a fetter on the unjust. She smooths rough places, checks satiety, dims insolence, withers the flowers of folly as they spring; she straightens crooked judgments, softens the deeds of arrogance, checks the works of schism and factions,

1. Theognis, I, 143 ff.
2. Diehl, *Anthologia Lyrica* I; Solo, 3, 32 ff.

checks the gall of bitter strife, until beneath her rule all human life is harmonious and wise.

The derivation of his ethics from Hesiod is clear, as is the dependence of Theognis on Solon, from whom Theognis adapted various passages.[3]

Solon's endeavors to remove the injustices of the Attic law and to establish an orderly economic and political government give his poetry a vividness and vitality which are lacking in the verse of the "injured and venomous aristocrat,"[4] Theognis. The Athenian poet gives the reader the sense of the reality of his love of justice and law (Eunomia), and, as Linforth[5] has noted, his imaginative power expresses itself in vigorous and simple metaphors drawn from everyday life and from nature. But not even anger and a desire to "drink the blood of his enemies" and to "trample on the people and smite them with a sharp goad" can enliven the dull verse of Theognis. He is an advocate of his own caste rather than his country. Because of its didactic and gnomic character his work is called by Isocrates[6] "a counselor for human life." But it is a worldly and cynical wisdom that is imparted by Theognis. Isocrates, doubtless, did not include the erotic second book in his commendation of the work as a moral guide. Theognis appears as the representative of his social class rather than an individual, while the wise Solon who discourses with Croesus in the pages of Herodotus corresponds in spirit to the Solon who is revealed in his poems.[7]

Solon is a pious man and believes, as Hesiod does, in the holiness of justice and in the righteous judgment of Zeus. He compares the vengeance of Zeus on the insolent man to

3. E. Harrison, *Studies in Theognis*, pp. 106 ff. Cambridge, 1912. For the influence of Theognis on Pindar and Bacchylides, *ibid.*, pp. 314 ff. Wilamowitz-Moellendorff, *Sappho und Simonides*, pp. 269 ff. Berlin, 1913.

4. M. Rostovtzeff, "The Orient and Greece," *History of the Ancient World*, p. 242. Oxford, 1930.

5. I. M. Linforth, *Solon the Athenian*, p. 121 f. University of California, Berkeley, 1919.

6. *Ad Nicoclem*, 43, 44.

7. Wilamowitz, *op. cit.*, pp. 11 f.

the wind that rises of a sudden in the spring-time, scattering the clouds, stirring the depths of the billowing, barren sea and ravaging lovely fields throughout the fruitful earth; it comes to the high dwelling of the gods in heaven and again discloses the bright sky. The sun shines fair upon the rich earth and no longer is there any cloud in sight.

He prays to the Muses that he may be given prosperity and fame, that he may be a joy to his friends and gall to his enemies. It is honest wealth that he desires and he condemns the misuse of riches. He sees the uncertainties of human life and endeavor, and acquiesces in the will of Zeus.

Theognis, on the contrary, in one of his most notable passages,[8] reproaches Zeus for treating the bad man and the good man alike, and for giving wealth to the wicked and poverty to those who keep their hearts from baseness.

The thoughtfulness and vigor of Solon's verse are watered down and often given a cynical turn by Theognis in his adaptations of the Athenian poet. The petulance of Theognis and his reiteration of moral precepts becomes tedious and the effect of his poetry, which is almost devoid of beauty, is gloomy without being tragic. His work gives a picture of Greek party struggle and its evils that is of political and historical value. As for the dark and vicious side of his poetry, it has been said[9] that he sins in good company in the feudal vices of the sixth century, which appear also in verses of Solon and of Pindar.

From Solon and Theognis, not great poets, but of great political and moral significance, I go on to consider the ethical quality of a poet whose verse is so full of splendor and his genius so overpowering that, though his thought is not morally deeper than that of his immediate predecessors, the grandeur of his poetic expression is immeasurably above theirs. He is the greatest extant poet, with the exception of Sappho, between Homer and Aeschylus.

The Greek word for virtue, *arete*, is hardly a word of the

8. Theognis, 373 ff.
9. E. Harrison, *Theognis*, p. 257.

New Testament. Outside of the Petrine Epistles,[10] in which
there is one example in the first Epistle and two in the second,[11] it occurs once in the Epistle to the Philippians.[12] It
was never completely specialized in the ethical meaning and
in Pindar and Bacchylides it continues in the same meaning
that it had in Homer[13] of excellence of any kind, particularly
physical quality, swiftness of foot, and prowess in contests.
Pindar uses the word very often, nearly seventy times in the
Odes, and distinguishes between the excellence that comes
by birth and nature[14] and that which is acquired by study
and learning. "By native excellence a man is mighty, but he
who has learned is vain, blows hot and cold, takes no sure
step, but essays a thousand deeds of virtue with purpose un-
fulfilled." Pindar[15] lacks the deep ethical feeling of Aeschylus,[16] his almost exact contemporary. As a professional poet
writing odes required by rich young athletes and such despots as Hiero of Sicily, Theron of Acragas, the Aleuad
tyrants of Thessaly, and Arkesilas of Cyrene, he was bound
to praise in his songs success in the games, the splendor of
the tyrants, their opulence and power. He was aware and
proud of his genius and says of his own poetry, "He is the
true poet whose great knowledge comes from nature, but
those who have learned their art are noisy chatterers, crows
that caw foolishly in competition with the divine bird of
Zeus."[17]

His good taste forbids him to believe horrible stories about
the gods.[18] "It is fitting for a man to speak good things about
deities."[19] "To revile the gods is hateful artistry."[20] But it

10. I Pet. 2. 9; II Pet. 1. 3, 5
11. Generally acknowledged to be a second-century work.
12. *Phil.,* 4, 8.
13. *Il.,* XV, 622; XXIII, 276, etc.
14. *Nem.,* III, 40 ff. Cf. *Ol.,* IX, 100 f.; *op. cit.,* II, 86 ff.
15. 518–447 B.C.
16. 525–456 B.C.
17. *Ol.,* II, 86 ff.
18. *Ibid.,* I, 52.
19. *Ibid.,* I, 35.
20. *Ibid.* IX, 37.

is not against his code to ascribe to the gods a sin like sodomy, which was common in his own class and country, nor did any moral scruples prevent him from writing an ode[21] for Xenophon of Corinth when he presented the temple of Aphrodite in that city with one hundred temple-prostitutes, after he had won a victory at Olympia.

"Girls, who have many a guest, handmaids of Peitho in wealthy Corinth," etc.

His poems are full of piety and reverence for the gods and he is imbued with the Orphic doctrines of reward for the good and punishment for the evil man.[22] This Orphic teaching is found in his beautiful second Olympian ode.

Wealth, when set like a jewel in the midst of virtues, brings opportunity for this and that, keeping down carking care.[23] It is a bright star, a true light for a man, if the man who has it knows that which shall be, that the guilty souls of those that die, pay penalties; for all the sins committed in this realm of Zeus are judged by one below, who passes sentences by hateful necessity. But in sunlight, day and night alike, the good receive a life without toil; not harrowing the earth with the strength of their hands, nor vexing the water of the sea, they live a life where tears are not, with those honored of the gods, who have taken joy in keeping oaths, but the wicked suffer anguish on which eyes cannot bear to look.

Those who have ventured thrice to abide on either side of death, keeping their souls from all unjust acts, go the road of Zeus to Cronos' tower. There the ocean-breezes blow about the islands of the blest and flowers glow with gold, some on the shore on shining trees and others nourished by the water. With crowns of these they wreath their heads and arms, by the righteous will of Rhadamanthus.

A famous fragment[24] gives an Orphic picture of the world of the blessed.

For them the strength of the sun shines below, while here it is night. On meadows red with roses the space before their city is

---

21. Pindar, *Frag.* 122.
22. *Ol.*, II, 53 ff.
23. Or "putting in the heart of man a deep and eager mood," Myers.
24. *Frag.* 129, 130.

full of shady frankincense-trees and golden fruit. Some take delight in horses and some in dice and some with the harp, and among them happiness with its fair flowers blooms. Through the lovely place there spreads the fragrance of incense of every kind, mingled and burning on the altars of the gods and sending its flame afar.

Pindar's love of material splendor finds expression in these pictures of material happiness in immortal life, "plainly Orphic doctrine, with beauty and distinction added to it by the genius of the great poet."[25]

Pindar has very many personifications, some of virtues. The triad of orderly virtues in Corinth, Eunomia, Dike, and Eirene,[26] I have already noted. Themis and her daughter Eunomia are said by him also to have their dwelling in Opus. His most beautiful personification of a gentle virtue is in his invocation to tranquillity, *Hesychia,* in the splendid eighth Pythian ode.

Kindly Tranquillity, daughter of Justice from whom the greatness of a city comes, thou who holdest the master keys of counsels and of wars, accept this honor to Aristomenes, won in the Pythian games. Thou dost know how to give and to take gentleness at the unerring moment; if any one conceives in his heart relentless wrath, thou dost face the might of the foe and dost hurl Insolence into the sea.

He praises Hesychia also in Fragment 109. "If a man strives to establish the commonwealth in sunlit calm, let him seek the bright face of strong Tranquillity and put malicious faction from his heart, for it bestoweth poverty and is a bitter nurse of childhood." Among his other personifications are the Goddess of Truth, daughter of Zeus, Aletheia, "no real figure in the world of Greek mythology and cult,"[27]

25. J. A. Stewart, *The Myths of Plato,* p. 68. London, 1905.
For Plato's debt to Pindar in Orphism, see pp. 66–71.
26. *Ol.,* XIII, 7.
27. *Ibid.,* X (XI), 4.
Cf. L. R. Farnell, *The Works of Pindar,* Critical Commentary, p. 79. London, 1930–32.
Frag. 205. "Foundation of all high virtue, Mistress Truth, let not my bargain strike upon the rock of lies."

the Goddess of Exactness, Good Faith, Atrekeia, who is said to make her home among the western Locrians;[28] Alala, the personified War-Cry,[29] "Hear, O Spirit of the War-Cry, Alala, daughter of battle, prelude of the spear-thrust. Thy sacrifices are men who for their land die the death of holy victims." Hesychia, daughter of Justice,[30] appears to be a cultless personification, as is Angelia, Goddess of News, daughter of Hermes,[31] and probably Euthymia, Goddess of Festivity.[32] Pindar is like Hesiod in expressing his ethical ideas in his personifications, which he often improvises on the spur of the moment.

It has been said of Pindar that he is one of the great poets who are without pity and without love.[33] It is true that he sees only the glory of the winning side and twice expresses in ugly language bitter scorn for the defeated, once in the eighth Olympian ode and again in the eighth Pythian. In a passage in each of these odes, to heighten the glory of the victor, he dwells on the way in which the vanquished competitor will be hissed and reviled by the crowds as he slinks home to his mother by some bypath, seeking to avoid the hostile outcry of his townsmen. The passage in the eighth Pythian ode, which reveals the Greeks for whom Pindar wrote as "such bad sportsmen,"[34] immediately precedes the wonderful lines—"In a brief moment the joy of mortals grows and falls to earth, cut down by adverse destiny. Creatures of a day! What are we? What are we not? Man is the dream of a shadow. But when the gleam of splendor comes, sent from God, a shining light encompasses him and life is sweet."

This "splendor sent from God" gives Pindar's ideal, splen-

28. *Ol.*, X (XI), 13 f.
29. *Frag.* 78.
30. *Pyth.*, VIII, 1 ff.
31. *Ol.*, VIII, 81.
32. *Frag.* 155. Represented on an amphora in Berlin. Roscher, I, 1438.
33. Mackail, *Lectures on Greek Poetry*, p. 120. London, 1910.
34. Farnell, *The Works of Pindar*. Translation with Literary Comments, pp. 46, 130.

did achievement celebrated in splendid song is to him the highest good that man can attain.[35] He utters reflections on the brevity of life, the changes of fortune, and the beauty of achievement that are expressed with the utmost magnificence, but with all his magnificence his range of thought is too narrow and he is too thoroughly and consciously an aristocrat by birth and intellect to be a great poet in the sense that Homer, the Attic dramatists, and Shakespeare are great. The Graces, his Boeotian goddesses, "by[36] whose aid all joy and sweetness is won for mortals, whether a man is a poet or has beauty, or a splendid life,"[37] gave Pindar every gift except that of touching the heart. Like his countryman Hesiod he is a notable moralizer and his didactic passages are often among his finest. I quote one such, addressed to Hiero, the great Syracusan dynast, in the first Pythian ode.[38]

Yet, since to be envied is far better than to be pitied, hold to high and noble aims. Govern your folk with the rudder of justice. Forge your speech on the anvil of truth. If any word, though trivial, flashes from you, it is held weighty, since it comes from you. You are the treasurer of great wealth, and many are witnesses to good and evil deeds. Abiding in a temper that bears fair blossoms, if you desire to hear men speak well of you, do not be niggardly in spending your riches, but put on full sail, like a ship-captain. Be not deceived by easy gain. It is the praise that lives after men that makes them known in story and in song. The kindly virtue of Croesus is never lost to memory while an evil report everywhere tells of Phalaris of pitiless heart, who burned men in the brazen bull. To achieve success is the first of prizes, to be famed is the next apportioned blessing. If a man meets and captures both, he has got the highest crown.

These verses exhibit Pindar's plainspeaking to princes, which his high position as panhellenic poet warranted; a

35. *Ol.*, V. 14 ff.; *Pyth.*, I, 99 f.; *Isthm, V* (IV), 12 ff.; *Pyth.*, X, 19 ff.; *Isthm.*, VI, 10 ff., *et pass.*

36. *Ol.*, XIV, 4 ff.

37. For the Boeotian Feast of the Graces, the *Charitesia* at Orchomenos, see I. C. Ringwood, *Agonistic Features of Local Greek Festivals*, pp. 39 f. Poughkeepsie, N. Y., 1927.

38. *Pyth.*, I, 85 ff.

remarkable instance of this is his plea for the return of the exiled Damophilus at the end of the fourth Pythian ode, addressed to King Arkesilas of Cyrene.

In this poet, who was the associate and poet laureate of kings and wealthy citizens of the various Greek states, we expect and find the praise of the aristocratic virtues of the young nobles, courage, strength, love of song and music, generosity in spending lavishly on the arts of poetry and sculpture, and hospitality; but the common virtues of sad humanity, and those which, as Aeschylus knew, "come by suffering,"[39] are almost completely lacking in Pindar's odes.

Though he is a friend of despots and irresponsible rulers, there is a passage in which he approaches the standpoint of Aeschylus in praising the middle class.[40] The ode has for its myth the treachery of Clytemnestra, and if those scholars who assign it to the year 454 B.C. are right, Pindar may have been stirred by the final trilogy of his great contemporary both in his use of the myth and in his enunciation of political views, which closely resembles *Eumenides*, 526 ff. Pindar says in the eleventh Pythian ode, "May I set my heart on noble things that come from God, seeking what is possible at my time of life. I find the middle estate flowers with greater happiness in the city and I have no praise for the lot of tyrants. I am eager for the excellences that are open to all."

This expresses political sentiment that one would think alien to Pindar, and echoes, if the date of the eleventh Pythian is 454 B.C., the song of the Chorus in the *Eumenides*,[41] "Neither life that is without rule nor the life ruled by a despot shalt thou praise. God looks on all things everywhere, but gives the power to the middle course always."[42]

39. Aesch., *Ag.*, 176 ff.   40. *Pyth.*, XI, 50 ff.   41. *Eum.*, 526 ff.
42. Cf. the beautiful and accurate poetical translation of Gilbert Murray.
     "The life that walketh without rule,
     The life that is a tyrant's fool,

     Thou shalt not praise.
     O'er all man's striving variously
     God looketh, but where'er it be
     Gives to tthe Mean his victory."

This coincidence in the praise of the middle course seems to me an added argument in favor of the date 454 B.C. (rather than 474 B.C.) for Pindar's poem.[43] The date of the Aeschylean trilogy is 458 B.C.

The poems of Pindar's two rivals, to whom he perhaps refers contemptuously in the second Olympian ode,[44] Simonides and Bacchylides, are much more simple and tender than those of Pindar. The two were uncle and nephew and came from the Ionian island of Ceos, near the Attic coast. Simonides, "the tenderest poet that could be,"[45] was much the oldest[46] of the three writers of victory odes and is the first recorded poet to write a poem of this kind. Only a small part of his work is extant, though his poetical career extended over a long period in the sixth and fifth centuries B.C. The most famous of his poems that remain is the lovely lament of Danae in the "ark," or chest, in which her angry father had set her afloat with her baby Perseus.

The sweet lulling song with which she quiets her child is lovelier and more tender than any other poem that has come down from antiquity.[47] Pindar could not have written it. Simonides is also famous for his epitaphs, especially those on the soldiers who died at Marathon, Thermopylae, and on other battlefields in the Persian Wars. He borrows[48] and adapts from Hesiod[49] that poet's famous passage in which Virtue is said to dwell upon a height, to which a difficult path leads, which man must sweat to climb. The passages in Hesiod and Simonides have a striking analogy in the New Testament.[50] In Hesiod Goodness is seated in a high place;

43. For a brief discussion of the date of the eleventh Pythian ode, see Farnell, *op. cit.*, Translation, pp. 148 f.

44. *Ol.*, II, 86 ff.

45. Wordsworth, Sonnet, *Simonides* (written in 1803.)

46. Simonides, 556–467 B.C. Pindar, 518–447 B.C. Bacchylides, 507–428 (?).

47. *Frag. 37.*   48. *Frag. 58.*

49. *W. and D.*, pp. 286 ff.

50. Matthew 7. 13 ff. Cf. Wilamowitz-Moellendorff, *Sappho und Simonides*, pp. 169–170, Berlin, 1913. "Sein Spruch über die zwei Wege, die der Mensch im Leben einschlagen kann, ist ein Grundstein der hellenischen Ethik geworden, und in das Evangelium übergegangen."

a steep and stony path leads to her, while Badness is easy of access, at the end of a level road. In the gospel of Matthew, Destruction has a broad and easy path leading to it, while the way upward to life is steep and narrow. The figure is that of "a gate opening into a road leading up to a citadel."[51]

Both Simonides and Bacchylides personify in the manner of Hesiod. The Lawgivers' triad of virtues, Eunomia, Dike, and Eirene—Order, Justice, and Peace—appears in a fragment ascribed to Simonides by Wilamowitz,[52] and the three are mentioned in various odes by the nephew.[53] Both poets personify Virtue,[54] the Greek word for which is, as Wilamowitz remarks, not a moral good in Hesiod, Theognis, Solon, and the lyric poets. Pindar employs the plural very often for "the activities in which the man born noble shows his nature, chiefly in the fulfilling of the duties that belong to his caste."[55]

Bacchylides has an interesting passage[56] in which he calls the highest virtue that of the righteous heart.

"There are countless excellences of men. One of these has the foremost place, that of him whose course is guided by a just heart, in all that he does." Here we have the standpoint of the Ionian thinker in contrast to the Dorian and Aeolian conceptions of the reactionary Theognis and of Pindar, lover of native and aristocratic virtues. Both Simonides and his nephew moralize the idea of "virtue" and advance it toward the ethical meaning attached to the word by Socrates and Plato. In the third Nemean ode Pindar speaks of four virtues, which life in its course brings on. These are believed to be the four virtues ascribed to Pythagoras and adopted by Plato. In the *Protagoras* of Plato, in which all these virtues are identified with and merged in knowledge, there

---

51. S. T. Bloomfield, *Greek Testament* (London, 1836), on Matthew, 7. 13.
52. *Isyllos von Epidauros*, p. 16. Berlin, 1886.
53. Bacchylides, VII, 186; XIV, 55; XII, 189, *Frag.* 3, 1; IV, 12.
54. Wilamowitz, *Sappho und Simonides*, p. 169.
55. Wilamowitz, *op. cit.*, p. 173 n. 1.
56. XIII, 8 ff.

is a discussion of a poem of Simonides, which attacks the saying of Pittakos that "it is hard to be a good man." Simonides declares that it is not merely hard, but impossible for a man to be perfectly blameless. He praises the man who does not of his own will commit a shameful act. Here Simonides introduces a new standard and definition for "good" conduct, and is on the way to a new ethical interpretation of "virtue."[57]

Bacchylides is doubtless using the word in the older sense of achievement, when he says:[58] "Virtue sending her light to all men, is never hidden or dimmed in the dusk of night, but burgeoning like a flower in unending beauty she goes to and fro over the earth and sea."

In the two Ionian poets, uncle and nephew, a deeper gravity and thoughtfulness about the conduct of life are evident in comparison with the Dorian and Aeolian writers of songs. Both Simonides and Bacchylides are imbued with the spirit of their neighbor, that Athens for whose dead Simonides wrote noble epitaphs—Athens, which in the lifetime of the two produced those tragedians of whom Matthew Arnold said that no other poets have ever lived so much by the imaginative reason and no others have so well satisfied both the thinking power and the religious sense.

I have spoken earlier of the pathos and beauty of Bacchylides' fifth ode and of the influence which it must have had on the plays which Sophocles and Euripides wrote on the fate of Meleager, and, through the fragments of Euripides and the résumé of the plot of his play by Apollodorus, on Swinburne's *Atlanta in Calydon*.

57. Wilamowitz, *op. cit.*, pp. 179 f.
58. XII, 175 ff.

VIII

THE INFLUENCE OF DEMOCRACY ON THE ETHICS
OF THE FIFTH CENTURY

Sophrosyne

"Where the sons of Athens laid the glorious foundation of liberty."

THESE words were written not by Aeschylus, the great poet of the New Democracy in Athens, but by the Theban Pindar, who in one ode[1] refers to democracy as "the turbulent mob." The verse is part of a famous fragment which won Pindar reward from Athens, but his city Thebes is said to have fined him for writing it. Three other lines of the poem are left: "Lovely, violet-crowned Athens, city renowned in song, the stay of Hellas, splendid Athens, marvelous city."

It is no wonder that Thebes did not like the poem and that the Athenians always rejoiced thereafter to call their city "the violet-crowned."[2]

Pindar knows the word "liberty," the watchword of the New Democracy, but he does not exult in the thought of it, as Aeschylus and Herodotus exult. He is a Theban, of the city that medized during the struggle with the Persians. He rejoices after that struggle was over[3] "that God has turned away the Tantalus stone that hung above the head of Hellas, a burden intolerable," but he has few references to Athens[4] in his odes and his sympathies are

1. *Pyth.*, II, 87.
2. Farnell, *Pindar*, I, 323 f. It is probable, though not certain, that the two fragments quoted above belong to the same dithyramb. See Farnell, *op. cit.*, p. 322.
3. *Isthm.*, VIII, 10 ff.
4. But cf. *Pyth.*, I, 76 ff. "From Salamis shall I get a meed of praise from Athens and from Sparta when I tell of the fight before Cithaeron, battles in which the Persians with crooked bows met disaster."

"with the Dorian laws of Aigimios."[5] The ecstasy[6] which Herodotus, a refugee from tyranny in Halicarnassus, felt for *isonomia,* equality of privilege, which he found in Athens, was utterly foreign to Pindar, even though the latter, once at least, took occasion to speak ill of tyranny. I quote in Gilbert Murray's translation[7] the vital words on the subject found in Herodotus, III, 80. "A tyrant disturbs ancient laws, violates women, kills men without trial. But a people ruling—first, the very name of it is so beautiful, Isonomiê (Equality in Law); and secondly a people does none of these things."

The first example of the word *demokratia* in literature occurs in Herodotus (VI, 43), but there is inscriptional[8] evidence from Chios of a democratic form of constitution in that island, about 600 B.C. Though the word *demokratia* does not occur in the inscription, the words δῆμος,[9] δημόσιος,[10] and δήμαρχος[11] all occur and the demos issues laws and is represented by its demarchs. Tod *(loc. cit.)* quotes Wilamowitz to the effect that the chief value of the document lies in the fact that it makes us realize that "the foundation for the organization of Greek society and the Greek state was laid in Ionia, exactly as for poetry and philosophy."

Professor Gertrude Hirst has shown in her admirable article[12] that Herodotus' third book is a tacit indictment of all tyranny and an encomium of the blessings of democratic government at Athens. As Socrates says in the *Gorgias*[13] that he is in love with philosophy, so Herodotus

5. *Pyth.,* I, 64.
6. Cf. Murray, *The Athenian Drama,* pp. xxiv ff. London, 1902.
Hirst, "Herodotus on Tyranny versus Athens and Democracy," in *Collected Classical Papers of Gertrude Mary Hirst,* pp. 97 ff. Oxford, 1938.
7. *Op. cit.,* p. XXIV.
8. M. N. Tod, *A Selection of Greek Historical Inscriptions,* pp. 1–3. Oxford, 1933.
9. People.
10. Of the people, popular.
11. Representative of the people.
12. *Op. cit.*
13. 481 B.

might well say, and does say often by implication, that he is in love with democracy.

It was this democratic policy of Athens that Pericles praised in his *Funeral Oration*,[14] and belief in this form of government has been recently reaffirmed by a distinguished visitor to this country, Dr. Eduard Beneš, lately President of Czechoslovakia: "Democracy is the inherent quality which makes man something higher than the beast, which lifts his heart to the stars and carries his soul onward and upward."

It was such a lyric and passionate love of and belief in democracy as this that inspired the poets and artists who celebrated in poetry and in bronze and marble the new era brought about by the death of one of the Peisistratidae and the expulsion of the others. The Athenians gave the credit for the whole complicated chain of events that brought them liberty to two men, whom they heroized, Harmodius and Aristogeiton—the two who, as Athens sang, "slew the tyrant[15] and made Athens free."[16]

The poet who felt most deeply and passionately the meaning of the new era was Aeschylus, who was born at Eleusis in 525 B.C., while the sons of Peisistratus were still the tyrants of Athens, and died in 454 B.C., when Pericles, a young man, had just begun his great career. We feel the thrill of Aeschylus' ardor for freedom in the proud words which describe Athens.[17]

Atossa. "Who is their master and who the despot of their folk?"

Chorus. "They have no master, they obey no king."

And again in the battle cry of the Greek fleet:[18]

14. Thuc. II, 35 ff.
15. 514 B.C.
16. The word for free is the adjective belonging with the word *isonomy*, which gave Herodotus such delight. It means "equal before the law." See Bowra, *Greek Lyric Poetry*, pp. 416 ff., for this Drinking-Song and a discussion of it.
17. *Persians*, 241 f.
18. *Ibid.*, 402 ff.

"O, sons of Greece, get freedom for your fatherland, your children and your wives, the temples of your fathers' gods, your fathers' tombs. It is for your all you fight."

The passages just quoted occur in the play entitled the *Persians,* written by Aeschylus about eight years after the Battle of Salamis.[19] Aeschylus had fought at Marathon and he fought on an Athenian ship[20] at Salamis. The Persian messenger in the drama, who reports the defeat to the Persian queen, Athosa, narrates the course of the battle with extraordinary fire and passion, in such detail that the *Persians* is a historical document of great value. The narrative, though spoken by a Persian, is full of Athenian sentiment and praise of Athens. Herodotus, much younger than Aeschylus and contemporary and friend of Sophocles, has the same spirit in his account of this battle and of the Persian Wars in general. His work has been called by that eminent authority, R. W. Macan,[21] "the noblest tribute ever laid at the feet of the violet-crowned Athens." We have no proof that the Aeschylean drama directly inspired the account of the battle given by the younger writer in the eighth book of his history, and while Herodotus must have known the *Persians,* he, of course, had many other written sources[22] and documents to draw on, and also other poets. "The debt of Herodotus to Aischylos is admitted, though it concerns the spirit rather than the letter."[23] Since the dramas of Aeschylus alone survive from the dramatic poetry of the early part of the century, it is easy to exaggerate the influence of the poet on the work of the historian. Yet, so far as we are able to discern, the spirit of the two seems so akin that it is difficult not to suppose that the first great

19. *The Persians* was produced in 472 B.C.
20. Schol. on Aesch., *Persae,* 429.
Paus., I, 14, 5.
Medicean Life of Aeschylus, p. 2.
21. *Camb. Anc. Hist.,* V, 410.
22. R. W. Macan, *Herodotus,* VII–IX, 74. London, 1908.
23. *Ibid.*

genius to write history was influenced by his older contemporary, the first great master of tragedy. Herodotus mentions the name of Aeschylus in a way that shows familiarity with his dramas. In his book about Egypt he says casually that Aeschylus, son of Euphorion, was the first to make Artemis a daughter of Demeter, getting the idea from the relationship of the Egyptian Isis and Boubastis.[24] He does not mention Aeschylus in his account of either battle, but does tell of his brother's[25] death in the Battle of Marathon. Kynegeiros, son of Euphorion, was among the many notable Athenians who were killed while attempting to board the Persian ships. The brother of Aeschylus is one of three men whose names are mentioned by Herodotus, who also tells the circumstances of his death.

So Herodotus knew the dramas of Aeschylus and records the bravery of his brother. At this distance of time and in the dearth of early fifth-century writing the influence of Aeschylus on the spirit of Herodotus seems great. "The Art of Tragedy," of which Aeschylus was virtually the founder, "was the product of democracy,"[26] and the art of the historian Herodotus was shaped by his hatred of tyranny and by his love for democratic Athens.

Though the two writers touch each other directly only in their respective accounts of the Battle of Salamis, they are at one in their moral outlook, in their hatred of *hubris,* the sin of insolent pride. This is the underlying theme of their work. Aeschylus is the greatest theologian that ancient Greece produced. He studies in his dramas the nature of God and the fate of man. Herodotus shows the working out in history of divine jealousy of human great-

24. *Hdt.,* II, 156, 137.
25. *Hdt.,* VI, 114.
26. G. Thomson, *The Oresteia,* p. 10. Cambridge, 1938.
Cf. the very interesting discussion of the relation of tragedy to democracy, pp. 10 f.
Also *id.,* "Social Origins of Greek Tragedy," *The Modern Quarterly,* I, Vol. 3, pp. 232–264. London, 1938.

ness, and, more deeply, how the pride of men brings them low, how, as St. Paul says,[27] "God chose the weak things of the world that he might put to shame them that are strong—that no flesh should glory before God." J. A. K. Thomson[28] says of the Jealousy of the Gods as a motive in the *Logoi* of Herodotus—

from the ordinary Greek point of view the gods did right to be jealous. It was their business as sovereign powers to punish any mortal who claimed their privileges; for it was only by a system of graded subordination that the world could be governed. . . . Zeus is the King and 'the King can do no wrong,' that was the feeling. Rooted in such a feeling, how could the doctrine of the Divine Jealousy be really moralized? Plato knew that it could not, and therefore in the great Myth of the *Phaedrus* Jealousy has no part in the harmonious company of the gods.

Aeschylus in one passage[29] denies "the ancient doctrine uttered long ago that misery is the offspring of prosperity." He says: "I have my own opinion, apart from other men. In truth the impious deed itself begets more evil, like to its own tribe. The fortune of the house that is ruled by justice is blessed in its fruits forevermore." He sees[30] that it is hard for a rich and powerful man to keep himself from sin, but he does not often mention divine jealousy, though he speaks of the dangers of excessive wealth and power.[31] The mention of the Jealousy of the Gods is so frequent in Herodotus that it is commonly associated with his religious ideas. The word for jealousy is *phthonos* and in Aeschylus there is the tendency to substitute *hubris*, the insolent sin of men, for the divine jealousy, as the cause of

27. I Corinthians 1.27, 28.
28. *The Art of the Logos,* pp. 149 f. London, 1935.
29. *Ag.,* 751 ff.
30. *Ibid.,* 471 ff.
31. *Ibid.,* 462 ff. Here he speaks first of the watch the gods keep on the murderer. Then come the lines about danger of too great glory, etc.

Ibid., 904. Clytemnestra speaks. Agamemnon says he fears the jealousy of the gods if he treads on purple. In these passages the characters utter "the commonplace of Greek morality that God is jealous of the exceptional man." J. A. K. Thomson, *op. cit.,* p. 123.

the downfall of the mighty. In the *Persians*[32] the Ghost of Darius says that the corpses of the Persians fallen at Plataea shall bear witness forever that a mortal should hold his heart from overweening pride. "For Insolence, when it flowers, bears a fruit of folly, from which is reaped a harvest of woe." A few lines further on Zeus[33] is said to be a chastiser of the boastful heart, but nothing is said here of his jealousy of human greatness. In Herodotus[34] such jealousy is ascribed to God or gods, or to the Divinity, and not to a particular god. The change of emphasis from the jealousy of the gods as a motive for the fall of Xerxes to his own *hubris* and that of the Persians is an advance in moralization, but in the minds of the common people the idea of the Jealousy of the Gods was strengthened by the overthrow of the Persians.[35] The belief that "God[36] chose the weak things of this world that he might put to shame the things that are strong" was realized before their very eyes when Xerxes, the Great King, was defeated, and his enormous and splendid army and fleet were dispersed. Apart from the primitive ascription of base human emotion to the gods, the doctrine of the divine jealousy of mortals, "'though crude theology,"[37] was not "irreligious," and the words of Artabanus, uncle of Xerxes—"God does not suffer another than himself to be proud"—closely resemble the words of St. Paul written in a very different setting, "the things that are despised did God choose . . . that no flesh should glory before God."

Whatever opinion Herodotus himself may have held concerning the Jealousy of the Gods, which is often mentioned in the speeches made by the characters who appear

32. *Pers.*, 818 ff.
33. *Ibid.*, 827 f.
34. *Hdt.*, I, 32, 1; III, 40, 2; VII, 46, 7; VII, 10, 5; VIII, 109, 3.
These statements about the Divine Jealousy all occur in speeches. Cf. J. A. K. Thomson, *op. cit.*, pp. 121 f.
35. Kern, *Religion der Griechen*, II, 261 ff.
36. I Corinthians, 1.27
37. J. A. K. Thomson, *op. cit.*, p. 122.

in his history, there is no doubt that he shared the Aeschylean hatred of *hubris* and his belief in punishment for sin. Very early in his history he has Croesus say:[38] "The Persians are naturally given to *hubris"* (here=insolent pride) and he associates this quality with tyranny, as Aeschylus does. The wickedness of *hubris* and the certainty of retribution are the leading motives in his history, as in the dramas of the tragedian.

Aeschylus calls the seer Amphiaraus "a self-controlled, just, good, pious man."[39] The first adjective, which I have translated "self-controlled," belongs with the noun *sophrosyne,* which had begun to displace the early word, *aidos,*[40] so important in the epic. *Sophrosyne* is the most characteristic virtue of the fifth century. Its spirit pervades the literature and the art of that great period. In the next century Plato [41] considers *sophrosyne* to be a harmony, whether in the individual or in the state, as well as a mastery over the lures of pleasures and desires, so that the better self rules the worse. This Greek virtue belongs to the ideal Athenian, and also, in one of its senses[42] at least, to the ideal Spartan. Thucydides calls Archidamus, the Spartan king and leader in the early part of the Peloponnesian War, "an intelligent and self-controlled man," and in the speech that he puts in his mouth the king praises his citizens for their self-control, using the word[43] repeatedly with reference to them.

38. *Hdt.,* I, 89.

39. *Septem,* 610.
He is also called "most temperate" (*v.* 568). In lines 593 ff. is the famous passage about the seer, which the audience is said to have applied to Aristides. (Plut., *Arist.* 3.) "He wishes not to seem, but to be the best, and he reaps a deep furrow in his mind, from which good counsels spring."

40. Gilbert Murray notes (*Greek Epic,*[3] p. 89) how little *aidos* meant to Plato and Aristotle. Aristotle regards it not as a virtue, but as a feeling. He has much to say about *sophrosyne,* which has no place in the *Iliad.*

41. *Republic,* 430 ff.

42. Cf. *Laws,* 710 A.

43. Thuc. I, 80, 84.

Plato in the *Laws*[44] ranks *sophrosyne* next to wisdom. "Wisdom has the first place among the goods that are divine; temperance of soul combined with reason has the second place; after these two, mingled with courage, justice would come third, and fourth courage." Here we have again, as so often in Plato, the four Pythagorean virtues.

The words *sophron,* self-controlled, moderate, and *sophrosyne,* self-control, moderation, are, like *metrios,* moderate, favorite words in Greek democratic states.[45] The virtue of self-control, avoiding of *hubris,* was a natural development in the new democracy after the expulsion of the tyrant family, and especially after the Athenian victory over the great power of Persia. The word often has the meaning of moral wisdom, as in that chorus in the Agamemnon, in which Aeschylus[46] gives the noblest conception of Zeus in all Greek literature.

"Zeus who puts mortals on the road to understanding, who established the law that a man must learn by suffering. The wound bleeds when a man sleeps, keeping his heart mindful of the hurt, and wisdom comes to men against their will."

As befits the century in which its use prevailed over that of the old *aidos,* it is more intellectual than *aidos* and more moralized than *phronesis,* thoughtful wisdom, and *sophia,* knowledge. Gilbert Murray[47] so well says of it:

The meaning of sophrosyne can only be seen by observation of its usage. It is closely related to that old Greek rule of μηδὲν ἄγαν, *Nothing too much,* which seems to us now rather commonplace, but has in its time stayed so many blind lusts and triumphant vengeances. It is something like Temperance, Gentleness, Mercy;

---

44. *Laws,* 631 C. In *Laws,* 710 A, Plato speaks of the philosophic identification of wisdom and temperance. Plato uses three words at various times for the virtue of wisdom—*phronesis,* intelligence, *episteme,* understanding, *sophia,* knowledge.

45. See Liddell and Scott, *Greek Lexicon* (new ed.) *s.v.,* μέτριος.

46. *Ag.,* 180.

47. *Greek Epic,*² p. 26.

sometimes Innocence, never mere Caution; a tempering of dominant emotions by gentler thought.

The word is of no importance in the epic. The adjective occurs once in the *Iliad*[48] and once in the *Odyssey*,[49] and the noun twice in the *Odyssey*[50] in the meanings of sensible, good sense. Gradually and in response to the increasing sensitiveness of the Hellenic peoples, especially the Athenians, to the claims of humanity and the social conscience, *sophrosyne*[51] enlarged its meaning and came to signify goodness in a sense to which *arete,* the general word for virtue, never attained.

This new, more intellectual conception helped to restrict the use and meaning of the older word *aidos.* The two words are found together. Thucydides represents Archidamus[52] as saying that *aidos* has the greatest share in *sophrosyne,* and as late as the New Testament the word occurs together with *sophrosyne* "with shamefastness and sobriety," in an admonition to women to dress modestly and quietly.[53]

There is hardly an instance of the word in the work of the Hellenistic historian, Polybius.[54]

Plato[55] speaks of Aidos as having been the "queen" (feminine of despot) of Athens at the time of the Persian invasion. He calls the quality "the most noble fear," and says that, because of it, a new love and patriotism sprang up in Athens, which enabled the Athenians to save their city and gave them liberty. As one opposed to the rule of the

48. *Il.,* XXI, 462.
49. *Od.,* IV, 158.
50. *Ibid.,* XXIII, 13, 30.
51. "Plato always tries to extend the scope of these virtues (i.e., courage and temperance) as widely as he can, while Aristotle's chief endeavour is to narrow them down to their most literal meaning." J. Burnet, *The Ethics of Aristotle,* p. 110. London, 1900.
52. Thuc. I, 84.
53. I Tim. 2.9. This is the only place in the N. T. where the word occurs.
54. Schultz, *op. cit.,* p. 103. For the rarity of the word in the Attic orators, with the exception of Antiphon, see Schultz, p. 101.
55. *Laws,* 698 B, 699 C.

mob he deplores the license of liberty, as he sees it in his own time, when it has lost Aidos.

Thucydides[56] once uses the word *sophrosyne* in the political sense of a moderate form of government, in the case of the people of the island of Thasos, who regained their freedom after overthrowing the oligarchy established by the representative of the Oligarchy of the Four Hundred in Athens. The Attic orators, who are exponents of democracy and love of Athens, regard *sophrosyne* as the characteristic of the good citizen, who is also described by the words *metrios,* preserving the "mean" in conduct, and *kosmios,* orderly, which is combined with *sophron* to describe the ideal citizen of the democracy.[57] That ideal, formed in the fifth century and first described by Aeschylus,[58] is called by the orators of the fifth and fourth centuries B.C., temperate, orderly, moderate, reasonable, patriotic, philanthropic. From the time of the Persian Wars to the end of the Athenian democracy the virtue most praised in their literature is this "moderation," which has supplanted the older *aidos* as the opposite of *hubris.*

I have sketched the development of this virtue through the fifth century and beyond because it is universally recognized as the most distinctively Hellenic of all the virtues. Euripides speaks for his race when he says:[59]

"I hold that there is nothing that surpasses Moderation, for this is always a comrade of good men." And this exaltation of *sophrosyne* and the enlargement of its meaning accompany in Athens the fear and hatred of tyranny and the exaltation and love of democracy.

J. A. K. Thomson has written an enlightening and elo-

56. VIII, 64. See Liddell and Scott, last ed., *s.v.* Thuc. applies the adjective "moderate" to "aristocracy"; *i.e.* the aristocratic form of government, in III, 82, 8.

57. Lys., XXI, 19.

58. *Septem,* 610.

59. *Frag.* 959.

quent chapter on *sophrosyne*.[60] I quote from the closing paragraph.

Sophrosyne is the virtue that "saves"[61] in this battle. Understand it so, and you must share some part of the ardor this word inspired. It means the steady control and direction of the total energy of a man. It means discipline. It means concentration. It is the angel riding the whirl-wind, the charioteer driving the wild horses. There is no word for it in English, and we must coldly translate "modera-tion," "temperance," self-restraint. Moderation as a name for this strong-pulsed triumphant thing! Why even the late-born, unromantic Aristotle, even while he is describing Sophrosyne as a "mean" between excessive and deficient emotionality, turns aside to remark, as a thing almost too obvious to need pointing out, that "there is a sense in which Sophrosyne is an extreme."

This virtue was the gift of democracy to Athens in the years of which Pericles could say with just pride: "We love Beauty with thrift, and we love knowledge without softness."

60. *Greeks and Barbarians*, pp. 105–121. London, 1921.
61. Cf. Aristotle's etymology, *Ethics*, 1140b, 13.

IX

HUMANITY IN GREEK TRAGEDY
AESCHYLUS

"The tragic pleasure is that of pity and fear, and the poet has to produce it by a work of imitation."[1]

GREEK tragedy for us begins with the *Suppliants* of Aeschylus and ends with the *Iphigenia in Aulis* of Euripides, produced after the poet's death. The period is about ninety years. There were tragedians before Aeschylus and after Euripides. Their works are lost and it is probably not to call the inaccessible grapes sour to say that it is for literature no great loss—not great, certainly, in comparison with the loss of the plays of the fifth century, especially those of the three great dramatists. We have thirty-three tragedies and many fragments; seven complete tragedies composed by Aeschylus, seven by Sophocles, eighteen certainly by Euripides, and one that may be by Euripides, or by a later writer.

These tragedies represent the greatest height that Greek poetry attained in beauty and intellectual content. To some who are not familiar with the development of Greek thought and art, the subjects of these tragedies seem inhumane and horrible.[2] They are chiefly taken from the traditional stories about great families such as the House of Atreus, stories which Aristotle[3] says must be kept as they are in plot, though the poet may discover for himself the right way of treating them. And to heighten the tragic

1. Aristotle, *Poetics*, 1453b. Bywater's translation.
2. Cf. H. G. Wells, *The New Machiavelli* (4th ed.), p. 76. "The telling of incomprehensible parricides, of inexplicable incest, of gods faded beyond symbolism, of that Relentless Law we did not believe in for a moment, that no modern western European can believe in.—No Gilbert Murray had come as yet to touch these things to life again."
3. *Poetics*, 1453b.

effect, he says, the poet should seek for the tragic deed done within the family, such as the murder of Agamemnon by Clytemnestra, and of Clytemnestra by Orestes. "The Plot, in fact, should be so framed that, even without seeing the things take place, he who simply hears the account of them shall be filled with horror and pity at the incidents; which is just the effect that the mere recital of the story in *Oedipus* would have on one."

The modern thinker, Wells, finds the atrocities of the plots the most striking phenomenon in the Greek dramas. Their old critic, Plato, who wished to have the performance of tragedies on the stage forbidden in his ideal city, objected to the element of pity, which both he and Aristotle consider the principal emotion aroused by tragedy.[4] The "incomprehensible parricides" and "inexplicable incests," though by no means as numerous as Wells's sentence suggests, occur in certain plays, the most famous of which is the *Oedipus Tyrannus* of Sophocles. The incest is done in ignorance—it is part of the old folktale or legend,[5] and the extraordinary decency of the Greek tragedy in comparison with much of the drama of later times has often been noted. There are wicked women in Greek tragedy, Clytemnestras and Medeas, but not indecent women. Euripides is accused by Aristophanes of first bringing on the stage women in love. All this has been discussed with such wit and understanding by Gilbert Murray that there is no longer any need to explain or apologize for the Euripidean heroines.[6]

But much more important than the question of the plots is the question raised and answered to his own satisfaction by Plato, whether the tragic element of appeal to

4. Plato, *Republic*, 605 D ff.
Aristotle, *Poetics*, 1452a, 1453a.
5. Robert, *Oedipus*, pp. 44 ff. Berlin, 1915.
Jocasta originally the Earth-mother. Cf. G. Murray, "Hamlet and Orestes," *Classical Tradition in Poetry*, pp. 232 ff. London, 1927.
6. G. Murray, *Euripides and His Age*, pp. 33 f., 85 ff., *et pass*. London and New York, 1913.

pity is a softening and corrupting influence. He[7] blames the poets for satisfying by the spectacle of sorrow that part of us which has been starving for the opportunity of weeping and indulging itself with tears and lamentations. He argues that after nourishing the principle of pity by letting it feed on the sorrows of others we shall be the more disposed to self-pity and will be unable to control ourselves in our misfortunes. Aristotle answers this argument in the *Poetics* by the single phrase—"providing an outlet for such emotional states." Plato wishes to repress emotions in the interest of morality, Aristotle wishes to give them a proper outlet through tragedy, for the good of the soul. This is needed, he says elsewhere,[8] by the tenderhearted, those inclined to be afraid, and, in general, the emotional. Plato regards tragic pity as a poison for the soul. Aristotle considers it as a means of healing.[9] Puritan against his desire, for he confesses that he is under the spell of tragedy,[10] Plato, on the whole, is worsted in the argument, according to the theories prevailing in these days of psychoanalysis,[11] even though the world of scholarship still disputes about the exact meaning and merit of Aristotle's statement.[12]

Neither Plato nor Aristotle suggests directly that the tragedians wrote with a moral purpose. That was, however, generally understood, since Greek poetry had always been a means of instruction as well as of delight. "We make the men in the cities better by our wise admonitions," is said by Euripides in the *Frogs* of Aristophanes.[13] The poet was expected to give good instruction.

7. *Republic*, 606 B, C.

8. *Politics*, 1341b, 32. See Bywater, *Aristotle and the Art of Poetry*, pp. 159 ff., Oxford, 1909, for the discussion of Aristotle's theory of the cathartic effect of tragedy on the emotional part of the soul.

9. *Politics, loc. cit.*

10. *Republic*, 607 C.

11. See Cornford on Aristotle and Freud, quoted by G. Murray in *Classical Tradition in Poetry*, pp. 56 f.

12. See Lucas, *Tragedy*, pp. 26 ff. *The Emotional Effect of Tragedy*.

13. Aristophanes, *Frogs*, 1009 ff. See Plato, *Republic*, 606 E, for the common Greek opinion that Homer's poem taught morals and politics.

Aristotle, indeed, does say that the subject that is represented in tragedy should be worthy, and that the characters
should be good; that is, on a high level. The hero, according to his longest discussion of this point,[14] should not
excel in virtue or uprightness, but be like the average man,
between the perfectly good and the base: "For pity is
occasioned by undeserved misfortune, and fear by that of
a man like ourselves." He says that a good man must not
be seen passing from happiness to undeserved misfortune,
that he must lose his happiness through some error of
judgment, not because of any baseness or depravity. Tragedy,
he says, is an imitation not of individuals, but of life.[15]

Such a picture of life must have contained from its first
stumbling beginnings, as Pickard-Cambridge[16] says, elements
of solemnity. After it assumed its grand form[17] in the
dramas of Aeschylus, it became a great art and a noble
expression of ethical thought.

I have recalled the ancient difference[18] between Plato
and Aristotle about the value of poetry in order to bring
out the emphasis which both philosophers place on the
element of pity in tragedy, Plato finding this a weakness
and a corrupting influence, Aristotle regarding it as health-
ful and advantageous. Aristotle seems to have taken up the
challenge issued by Plato[19] to defend poetry in prose.

In the tragedies of the fifth century B.C. the great ethical
problems that occupied the inquiring minds of the Greeks

14. *Poetics,* 1453a.
Cf. 1448a, 4, 18. Aristotle is not consistent in what he says about the hero,
and sometimes demands that he be better than the average man. It was
difficult for him to generalize briefly about so many heroes and heroines.
15. *Poetics,* 1450a, 17.
16. A. W. Pickard-Cambridge, *Dithyramb, Tragedy and Comedy,* p. 219.
Oxford, 1927.
17. *Poetics,* 1449a, 21.
18. Cf. *Republic,* 607 B.
19. *Republic,* 607 D. Aristotle may have had in mind Plato's antithesis
between philosophy and poetry when he says *(Poetics* 1451b, 5–6) that poetry
is more philosophical and a more important thing than history, because its
statements are universals, and not particulars.

are presented and solved or not, according to the mind of the poet. Aeschylus has his answer in his "learning by suffering." He is sure that justice will in the end prevail and that insolence and violence will perish. In the early play, the *Suppliants,* the violence of the Egyptian suitors is for the moment checked, and the question of the expediency for Argos of receiving the refugees—a question that often faced Athens,[20] as it faces every civilized country in the world today—is settled in favor of the suppliant girls. The king is in a dilemma.

> How can I help ye without harm[21]
> To Argos; yet how spurn such prayers as these?

But he calls upon his people (v. 518, a democratic touch; cf. 601) and they vote to protect the daughters of Danaus. The drama is the first play of a trilogy, the other two plays of which are lost. From their fragments and from the account given in *Prometheus Bound* it seems probable that, besides the dramatization of the legend, a moral theme was the working of the mysterious will of Zeus, according to which the sufferings of Io and her descendants, the Danaids, shall result after many generations in the birth of a savior-hero, Heracles,[22] a descendant of the Danaid, Hypermnestra, who spared her cousin-husband. The drama demands from us compassion and sympathy for the fifty girls who are the heroines and form the chorus, fear for their safety, and anger against the *hubris* of the fifty pursuers, the Egyptian suitors, and the insolence and violence of their herald. In the choruses and speeches is revealed the mind of Aeschylus, searcher after God, lover of justice, and, like all the great minds of his generation except Pindar, a lover of the New Democracy. The cry of the maidens to Zeus,[23] "Keep from

20. Euripides, *Heraclid.* pp. 329 ff.; Thuc., I, 2, 6; II, 39; 1; Plutarch, *Solon,* XXIV.
21. *Suppliants,* 377–378, Gilbert Murray's translation.
22. Aeschylus, *Prometheus Bound,* 850 ff. Cf. *Suppliants,* 580 ff.
23. *Suppliants,* 528.

us the violence of men, which is abhorred by Thee," gives the feeling of the drama, and is thoroughly characteristic of the poet to whom *hubris* was the sin of sins, who wrote about it those magnificent and famous lines in the *Persians,* which I have already quoted.[24]

"The Danaids themselves, the virtual protagonists, are, after the manner of their sex, prayerful, trustful, despairing, grateful, reproachful, resolute, as circumstances change." Thus Tucker,[25] who sees that the character drawing in their case is true and natural. A recent writer[26] notes how extraordinary a thing it is that women in tragedy from Aeschylus to Ibsen dominate the situation and take the initiative. These girls are forerunners of all the dominating women of Attic tragedy from Clytemnestra and Antigone to Iphigenia. They force the king's hand by threatening, if he refuses to protect them, to hang themselves by their girdles to the statues of the gods at whose altars they are crouching, and so bring pollution on the land. It is really they who save the day. And the next (lost) play[27] showed them fiercely barbaric in their vengeance on their husbands. Their act of violence met its punishment, and the one sister who loved and held her hand from murder was acquitted by a court in which Aphrodite presided.

In the *Persians* the sin of *hubris* is dramatically presented in the most startling instance of it that Athens had seen. The poet's greatness of mind leads him to give a sympathetic picture of the defeated side and the anguish of the Persians, as well as a picture of the victory that meant freedom for Athens.

In the *Seven against Thebes* the theme is the City at War.[28] The sons of Oedipus fight one another for the throne and kill another. The Chorus laments for the twain who

24. *Persians,* 821 f.
25. T. G. Tucker, *Suppliants* of Aeschylus, p. 20. London, 1889.
26. Lucas, *Tragedy,* pp. 116 f.
27. *P. V.,* 850 ff. The plot of the two plays is given in these lines.
28. G. Murray, Introduction to translation of the *Seven against Thebes.*

"battered down walls, beheld a bitter single sway and ended their strife with the sword." "A bitter ender of strife is the stranger who came by sea, the sword forged in the fire, evil divider of goods, who fulfils the curse of the father."

Although Aristophanes[29] represents Aeschylus priding himself on the *Seven against Thebes* as a "drama full of the war god," which made men eager to fight, Aeschylus is not a lover of war in this or in any of his dramas.

It was the curse of Oedipus that brought strife between his two sons and caused the war against Thebes, a curse which his sons could not escape. Aeschylus wrestled with this problem of an inherited curse and the power of an evil inheritance to work on to the ruin of the race. It troubled his soul, as the problem of sin troubled the soul of St. Paul.[30] Both found refuge in the inscrutability of a Divine Will in which both believed.

The description of the seer Amphiaraus, the self-controlled, just, good, pious man,[31] suggests the four virtues so often named in Plato,[32] with the exception of *phronesis* or *sophia*, wisdom. Here "pious" is substituted for "wise," since it was "against his better thought,"[33] that the seer had joined Polynices in his attack on his native city. The third adjective, good, often means brave when used to describe a man. Piety is considered as justice toward the gods and part of *dikaiosyne*.[34] These four (or five) virtues, as I have said, form the ideal of the Athenian writers of the fifth and fourth centuries B.C. There is a tendency for some

29. *Frogs,* 1021 f.

30. Cf. *Suppliants,* 86 ff. "Zeus the inscrutable," with *Romans,* XI, 33, 36. "His ways past finding out."
Cf. *Ag.,* 160 ff., 1485 ff., "It cometh by Zeus, the cause of all, the doer of all," with Romans, 11.33; 9.21.

31. *Septem,* 597.

32. Plato, *Protagoras,* 361 B.

33. T. G. Tucker, *The Seven against Thebes of Aeschylus,* p. 125, n. on v. 597. Cambridge, 1908.

34. Cf. Plato, *Republic,* 442, 443. *Euthyphro* 11 E.

one virtue, *sophrosyne,* or wisdom, or justice, to absorb the others and at the end of the discussion in Plato's *Protagoras* Socrates has shown that all virtue is knowledge, here called *episteme.*[35] In the fourth book of the *Republic* Plato holds that "all virtues meet in justice" and that the true unity of virtue consists in justice, not in *sophia* (as the historical Socrates held *(Mem.* II, 9, 5)).[36]

Again *sophrosyne* seems to lead all the rest, as the most civilized virtue. So in the great Zeus chorus of the *Agamemnon* (176–183) it is the equivalent of wisdom learned by suffering and by thought.[37] In different moral moods one or another of the four virtues is exalted by the Greek poets, but in none is any one virtue more nobly exalted than *sophrosyne* by Aeschylus.

In the trilogy of the *Oresteia,* which so greatly advanced the Greeks "on the road to thought,"[38] Aeschylus puts on the stage in noble drama the problem of sin, avenged by sin, in seemingly endless succession, but finally robbed of its sting and annihilated by the vote of the Areopagus with the help of Apollo and of Athena, who acts in obedience to Zeus.[39] In these three plays, *Agamemnon, Choephori, Eumenides,* the last work of his life,[40] the poet gave a higher and nobler conception of Zeus than any that had yet been set forth; he discussed the problems of evil and good and paid tribute to the city and the democracy which he loved and had helped to establish. It has been said that it cannot be maintained that Aeschylus has solved the mighty problems that he raises.[41] He has raised them more poignantly

35. *Prot.* 361 B.

36. Adam, *The Republic of Plato,* I, 242 n. on l. 21. Aristotle, *Ethics,* 1129b, 25 ff.

37. Cf. G. Thomson, *The Prometheus Bound,* p. 12. "The virtue of *sophrosyne* is the highest of the virtues and we know that, in order to attain it, man must travel the path of suffering."

38. *Ag.,* 176 f.   39. *Eum.,* 826.

40. But cf. G. Thomson, *Prometheus Bound,* p. 38 ff., Cambridge, 1938, who gives some reasons for believing that that play was composed in the last two years of the poet's life.

41. Adam, *The Religious Teachers of Greece,* p. 154.

than anyone before him, and no one else in the centuries since he asked these questions has succeeded in answering them. Cornford[42] says so well of the effect of the *Agamemnon:* "The curtain lifts for a timeless moment on the spectacle of human life in an aspect known to the all-seeing eyes of Zeus; and when it drops again, we turn back to the mortal tragedy of Agamemnon and Clytemnestra, enlightened, purified, uplifted, calm."

In the *Prometheus Bound,* first play of a trilogy of which the other plays are lost, we have the most extraordinary of Greek dramas. The Titan hero is the savior of mankind. Aeschylus has taken the primitive story of Prometheus told by Hesiod and has motivated his theft of fire by his love and compassion for the human race. The presentation of Zeus as a tyrant bent on the destruction of mankind is so startling in comparison with the conception of that god in the other plays, especially in the *Agamemnon,* that the discrepancy has puzzled all thoughtful readers. The reasonable explanation is that Zeus, too, as well as men, learns by suffering and by degrees.[43] This, though it shocks some modern writers, would not seem irreligious to the Greeks, who were familiar with the idea of gods with human frailties, and believed in a succession of divine rulers, in which Zeus had reached the throne after two others had been expelled from it.[44]

42. *Thucydides Mythistoricus*, p. 145. Oxford 1924.
43. Cf. Thomas Hardy's Poem to the "Unknown God."
> "Haply Thy ancient rote-restricted ways
> Thy ripening rule transcends;
> That listless effort tends
> To grow percipient with advance of days
> And with percipience mends."

Cf. *P. V.,* 35, 186 f.
44. *Ag.,* 168 ff.
> "One there was who reigned of old,
> Big with wrath to brave and blast,
> Lo, his name is no more told!
> And who followed met at last
> His Third-thrower, and is gone."
> Gilbert Murray's translation.

There have been many discussions of this matter and I shall not go into it further, except to say that no doubt the religious and theologically minded poet found the way in the suceeding plays of the trilogy "of reconciling the Champion with the Oppressor of mankind,"[45] though Shelley was so averse to that idea.

In this play Zeus is the example of *hubris* and Prometheus is *philanthropos,* the lover of mankind. This word, destined to have so long a history, makes almost its first appearance in this play. It is used twice, and both times in a reproach to Prometheus for his philanthropic spirit.[46] In the orators and prose writers the word in various combinations describes the good citizens. It is essentially a democratic word, as appears from its combination with *demotikos,* democratic, of the people, a significantly Athenian word. Xenophon[47] calls Socrates "democratic and philanthropic"; i.e., a friend of mankind. Demosthenes brings out the meaning of the two words in the following passage.[48] "For the laws ordain nothing that is cruel or violent or oligarchic, but on the contrary, all their provisions are made in a democratic and philanthropic spirit."

It is notable that Prometheus has no word of reproach for the race which he has saved, for whose sake he suffers.

> I cast no blame on man, I do but crave[49]
> To show what love was in the gifts I gave.

He has only compassion for "the weak and dreamlike impotence in which the race of man was shackled."[50] He sets above all things his pity for mortals.[51]

---

45. Shelley, Introduction to *Prometheus Unbound.*
46. It appears near the beginning of the play, as though to give the keynote. In v. 11, Might, henchman of Zeus, speaks insultingly of the philanthropy of Prometheus, and in v. 28 the phrase is repeated by the Fire-God. Prometheus is taunted for his devotion to the wretched beings who so disgust Zeus that he wishes to annihilate them.
47. Xen., *Mem.,* I, 2, 60.
48. Dem., 707, 4, 20–25.
49. *P. V.,* 445 f., Gilbert Murray's translation.
50. *P. V.,* 547 f. (words of the Chorus)   51. *Ibid.,* 239.

The play is full of pity. The chorus of sea maidens, who have come from their sea caves in curiosity to know what the sound of hammering means, weep as they see their Titan brother-in-law crucified in agony, and they utter words of sympathetic grief. There is a wonderful chorus[52] in which all nature lifts her voice in lamentation for the sufferings of the savior-hero. The earth and all its peoples cry out in grief, the surges of the ocean rise and fall in lamentation, the depths of the earth are shaken and make moaning, and the sources of the rivers pour forth streams in pitying sorrow.

The *Prometheus* is the least dramatic and the grandest of all extant Greek dramas. It must have contributed largely to the moralization of religion in the fifth century B.C. Whatever the nature of the reconciliation in the final play, in which Prometheus was established as a triumphant god of civilized arts, worshiped with Hephaestus and Athena near Colonus,[53] the Athenians realized from the teaching of Aeschylus that even Zeus must be no tyrant and that this new ruler must acquire the "democratic" virtues of *sophrosyne* and justice.[54] Prometheus himself is "a personification of human intelligence, of human craft in vain war with higher powers."[55]

The grandeur of the play and its boldness of thought have influenced great, thinking minds such as Goethe and

52. *Ibid.*, 406–435.
53. Sophocles, *O. C.*, 54 ff.; Pausanias I, 30, 2–4. (The altar of Prometheus was in the Academy.)
   Cf. Shelley, *Promttheus Unbound*, Act III, sc. iii.
      It is deserted now, but once it bore
      Thy name, Prometheus; there the emulous youths
      Bore to thy honour thro' the divine gloom
      The lamp that was thine emblem; even as those
      Who bear the untransmitted torch of hope
      Into the grave, across the night of life,
      As thou hast borne it most triumphantly
      To this far goal of Time.
54. Plato, *Republic*, 500 D, "Self-restraint and justice and the whole of democratic (or popular) virtue."
55. E. R. Bevan, *Prometheus Bound of Aeschylus*, p. 23. London, 1902.

Shelley. In his old age Goethe[56] feared that his own youthful *Prometheus,* written fifty years before, might appear as a gospel to the "revolutionary youth" of 1820 and set their inflammable minds on fire. He desired the suppression of the play, which he says, might bring him trouble from the authorities at Berlin and Mainz.

It is not the fashion, as it was formerly, to regard Prometheus as a guilty sinner, responsible for all the pain and misery of life.[57] It is no longer generally held that "the unbiased observer cannot but feel the character of Zeus to be the higher and nobler."[58] Rather, Aeschylus has presented in this play a picture of the civilizing of primitive men by one who loved them, in spite of their weakness, and saved them all from destruction, not merely an elect few.

> Behold how in an ancient heart rose up
> This vision of the wise, kind god, who viewed
> Naked and poor, in bondage of blind pain,
> Man's tremulous brood, nor longer would retain
> His blissful seat, but drank a bitter cup,
> Having compassion on the multitude.[59]

56. Goethe's *Werke* (Weimar ed.), XXXIII, 27 ff. *Briefe,* 1820 (letter to C. Fr. Zeller).
57. So Wecklein, *Prometheus,* translated by F. D. Allen, p. 7.
58. *Ibid.,* p. 11.
59. Bevan, *Prometheus Bound of Aeschýlus.*

X

RELIGION VERSUS HUMANITY IN SOPHOCLES
THE UNWRITTEN LAWS

No one is wise but the man whom God honors.
Even if thou art bidden to proceed
Apart from right, thou must needs go on.
For nothing is disgraceful which the Gods initiate.[1]

CONTRASTING the tone of this Sophoclean fragment with that of Euripides' famous line (*fr.* 272, 7), "if gods do anything disgraceful, they are not gods," A. C. Pearson says of the respective attitudes of Sophocles and Euripides toward morality and religion:

"Sophocles[2] is serenely confident that no reconciliation of their claims is necessary; if morality seems to conflict with the will of the gods,[3] so much the worse for it. But for Euripides, if the gods seem to enjoin an immoral action, they become untrue to their nature and are no longer trustworthy."

The contrast between the demands of religion *(eusebeia)* and those of human morality in several of Sophocles' plays, above all in the *Oedipus Tyrannus* and the *Electra*, must have been felt by many thinking Athenians when the plays were produced. Euripides appears to react against the Sophoclean standpoint in some of his extant plays; Aeschylus had always kept the belief that sin was punished in the end; Sophocles, holding the same belief, dwells upon the theme of the innocent man or woman, who is doomed by

1. A. C. Pearson, *The Fragments of Sophocles*, I, 187 f. *Frag.* 247. Cambridge, 1917.
2. Cf. E. Rohde, *Psyche* (8th ed.), translated by W. B. Hillis, pp. 428 ff. New York, 1925. "He himself is one of the pious—who feel no need that this mighty will (of the gods) should prove itself such (*i.e.,* holy) at the bar of human justice."
3. See Pearson, *op. cit.,* for the incest of Thyestes referred to in this fragment.

some ancestral sin, or by some involuntary error of judgment. He does not defend the gods, nor attempt to show that they are just in punishing the innocent.

Before everything else Sophocles is a dramatist, and, as he himself says, interested in character, at least during what he calls his final and best stage of development.[4] His gods have no especial character. They are the authors and the embodiment of the Eternal Laws, under which his innocent heroes and heroines suffer. To present human life and human suffering on the stage with all the power of his genius was his art and profession. He did this against a background of *eusebeia,* reverence for the gods, but his living interest was the tragedy that lies in the dissonances of human life.

The *Oedipus Tyrannus* resembles a tragedy of fate[5] and of that aspect of it one can say only that it represents life. Life is, or may be, like that. But if we are asked by the poet not only to acquiesce in the blows of fate, as men must, but also to admire and worship gods "strangely and incomprehensibly malignant,"[6] it seems that, for one reason or another, Sophocles refused to face the question of the morality and goodness of the gods, as Aeschylus and Euripides did not refuse. He is careful to praise the gods.[7] A scholium[8] calls him the most god-revering of men. But "a criticism of life, or any definite moral judgment,"[9] such as Euripides makes in his plays, is rare in Sophocles.

Was it devotion to his art and his dramatic sense, the desire to make the *Oedipus Tyrannus* overwhelming in its theatrical effect, or was it piety that kept him from any

---

4. Plut., *Profect. Virt.* 7.

5. E. E. Sikes, *The Greek View of Poetry,* pp. 142 ff. London, 1931. Schmid-Stählin, *Griechische Literatur-geschichte,* II, I, pp. 370–372. Munich, 1934.

6. Murray, *Oedipus,* p. VII.

7. Criticism of them by Hyllus, *Trach.,* 1266 ff. and by Philoctetes, *Philoctetes* 446 ff.

8. Schol. *Soph. El.* 831.

9. Murray, *op. cit.;* cf. Rohde, *op. cit.,* pp. 426–431; Nestle, "Sophokles und die Sophistik," *Classical Philology* V (1910), pp. 146 ff., 157.

arraignment of Apollo, such as Euripides did not shrink from making?

It has been said recently that in the *Oedipus* there is a triumphant justification of Apollo and his ministers, and that the play was written to combat the disbelief in the oracles which was so prevalent in Athens during the Peloponnesian War.[10] If the play is propaganda for Apollo, a "tract for the times," it failed to attain its purpose, for skepticism continued and increased, but it became what is immensely greater, one of the grandest and most shattering tragedies of human suffering that have appeared on any stage. Indeed, it is not unlikely that by its very power in the terrible depiction of an innocent man, helplessly entrapped by the oracles of Apollo, it contributed to the increase of contempt for and disbelief in the oracles. "It[11] was Apollo, Apollo, my friends, who brought to pass my bitter woes, my agony!" Many in the audiences who heard the cry of Oedipus must have felt with Euripides that an Apollo who could be so cruel did not exist at all, except in primitive religious imagination.

In answer to the question whether in the *Oedipus Tyrannus* Apollo is "playing a devilish game with mankind," Weinstock, who asks the question, replies that had Sophocles thought that, his play would be a tremendous accusation of God, a radical document of unbelief, whereas the pious songs of the Chorus, the triumphant vindication of the oracle at the end, and the suicide of the "godless Jocasta" prove that Sophocles was on the side of the god.[12] Weinstock declares that in the suicide of Jocasta "an incarnation of godlessness—a godless individual, pronounces judgment on herself." Such blindness to the true interpretation of Jocasta

10. T. B. L. Webster, *Sophocles*, p. 23, Oxford, 1936; cf. Nestle, *op. cit.*; cf. Weinstock, *op. cit.*, p. 178.

11. *O. T.*, 1329 f.

12. So also Webster, *op. cit.*, except that Webster does not condemn Jocasta. "Jocasta is like Deianeira in her quiet nobility and her love for her husband," *op. cit.*, p. 76.

is rare nowadays. She is no longer called "the arch-horror of the piece,"[13] or "a frivolous soul."[14] Her guilt, the casting away of her infant to save her husband's life, goes back to her early youth. It is not that sin, however, but her "blasphemies," that have shocked her critics. She believes in Apollo,[15] but casts doubt upon the art of expounding oracles. Her expressions of doubt are really desperate attempts to calm her husband at all costs.[16] Her last words, untranslatable in their anguish of grief, are the most tragic lines in Greek poetry.[17] As for Oedipus, his guilt was purely formal and ritual, since the stain upon him was incurred innocently; as he says, he was "a man more sinned against than sinning."[18]

I shall discuss later the song of the Chorus, O. T., 863 ff., which is believed to express horror at Jocasta's blasphemies and to state the poet's own belief in the sanctity and truth of oracles. Matthew Arnold quotes part of it to illustrate the union of the thinking power and the religious sense in Sophocles.[19] This song[20] is regarded as Sophocles' highest expression of piety, of that eusebeia, reverence toward the gods, which Heracles, in the Philoctetes, says Zeus places above all other things, "for piety does not die with mortals, and does not perish in life or death."[21]

Before considering further the apparent conflict between Greek religion and human standards of morality in Sopho-

---

13. L. Campbell, Sophocles, Plays and Fragments, I, 108. Oxford, 1871.

14. Robert, Oedipus, pp. 300 ff. Cf. Schmid-Stählin, op. cit., p. 364 n. 4, who notes Weinstock's entire misunderstanding of Jocasta. J. C. Collins, Studies in Shakespeare, p. 161, London, 1904, says, "Jocasta, coarse, reckless, and impious, expiates by her death little more than her life has earned."

15. O. T., 919 ff.

16. Schmid-Stählin, op. cit., p. 364 n. 4.

17. O. T., 1061, 1071 f.

18. O. C., 266 ff.

19. Critical Essays: Religious Sentiment, p. 145.

20. Nestle, op. cit., pp. 148 f., "ein Bekenntnis des Dichters." Schmidt-Stählin, op. cit., p. 370, n. 5.

21. Philoctetes, 1441 ff.

cles I will note some of the circumstances of his life and the subjects of his extant dramas.

Aeschylus died just as Pericles was coming into power and the *Oresteia*[22] is the latest work of his that was composed in the first half of the century and under the old, once the new, democracy. Over ten years later, when Sophocles was fifty-five years old,[23] he wrote his earliest extant play.[24] So the plays which we possess were written by a man in late middle life and in old age. He lived to be ninety years old and saw Athens in her height of glory and in her fall in the closing years of the Peloponnesian War. The *Ajax, Antigone,* and perhaps the *Oedipus Tyrannus* belong to the early part of this period, that is, between 441 B.C. and 429–428 B.C. The date of the *Trachinians* is disputable. I place it between 420 B.C. and 410 B.C.[25] The *Electra* (probably 415 B.C.) precedes the *Electra*[26] of Euripides, which is exactly dated to 413 B.C. by the reference in the speech of the *dei ex machina* at the end, to the movements of the Athenian fleet in Sicilian waters. The *Philoctetes* was produced in 409 B.C. and the *Oedipus at Colonus* was the work of his extreme old age.[27]

The period of the earlier plays was that called by the name of the great statesman, Pericles, who was a friend of Sophocles. In Thucydides' review[28] of the career of Pericles he says that Athens reached her greatest height while he was at the head of the government; that by his incorruptibility

22. If Professor George Thomson is right, the *Prometheus* was composed in the last two years of the poet's life. See Introduction to his edition of the *Prometheus Bound,* pp. 43 ff.

23. Shakespeare was but fifty-two when he died.

24. But E. Bruhn, *König Oedipus,* Berlin, 1897, dates the *Oedipus Tyrannus* in 456 B.C. His dating is not generally accepted.

25. G. H. Macurdy, *Chronology of the Extant Plays of Euripides,* pp. 61 ff. Also *Classical Review,* 25, 1911, pp. 97 ff.

26. *Id. Chronology of the Extant Plays of Euripides,* pp. 111 ff.

27. Sophocles lived 496–406 B.C.

28. Thuc., II, 65.

and statesmanship he exercised an enormous influence over
the multitude, never flattering them, but rather controlling
them in a free spirit; that they were aware of his high
character and obeyed him even when he rebuked them
harshly for arrogance or cowardice, and that the result was
that what was nominally a democracy was really a reign
of the first citizen.

It was in this Periclean democracy, which had become
the Athenian Empire, that the majority of Sophocles' more
than one hundred plays[29] were written. It was greatly
changed from that older democracy for which Aeschylus
fought and in which he wrote his stupendous dramas. In
them the problems of wickedness, retribution, the fall of
the proud, and of God's inhumanity to man (in the *Prometheus Bound*) are of more absorbing interest than the plots.
The interest in individual character, which emerges in
Eteocles in the *Seven against Thebes,* and to some extent in
the *Oresteia,* is developed by Sophocles, who has well-defined
human characters and plots. Aristotle, who loved a good
plot[30] and good handling of it, mentions Aeschylus very
seldom and takes no interest in his plays, while Sophocles is
for him the ideal dramatist and the *Oedipus Tyrannus* the
perfect play.

The Periclean Age was the age of the thinker about life,
religion, and morality, the age of the questioning sophists,
like Protagoras, who said that life was too short and the
subject too obscure to decide whether or not gods exist.
The mass of the Athenians were still conservative and
Protagoras was obliged to leave Athens. Persecutions for
impiety were frequent. Euripides[31] was prosecuted on this
charge by Cleon. Later he retired to the court of Archelaus
in Macedonia, Aspasia was charged with impiety, and
Pericles was obliged to send his friend, the philosopher

29. 114 titles of his plays are known; 130 are attributed to him. Pearson,
Sophocles' Fragments, I, XIII.
30. *Poetics,* 1450a.
31. Satyrus, *Pap. Oxyrh.,* IX, 153.

Anaxagoras, out of Athens.[32] The climax in punishments for opinion came in 399 B.C. when Athens put Socrates to death. Conservative Athens so resented being taught to think. The outbursts of heresy-hunting just before the beginning of the Peloponnesian War were both religious and political in origin and resulted directly from the bill[33] proposed by an interpreter of oracles, Diopeithes, for the impeachment of those who did not believe in the gods or taught natural science, astronomy, physics, etc. This proposal was aimed at Pericles and his friend Anaxagoras. The defense of oracles by Sophocles in the *Oedipus,* which has been held to be an attempt to stem the tide of skepticism in this respect,[34] would also be a defense of the anti-Periclean policy.

Sophocles was at one time an intimate friend of Pericles and was fellow-general with him at Samos in 441–440 B.C. If there are hostile references to Pericles in a chorus[35] of the *Oedipus,* as has often been suggested, it is possible that he was turned against the great statesman by the attacks made upon Pericles by the priestly party, who charged him and his friends with various degrees of impiety. Pheidias had carved likenesses of Pericles and himself on the shield of Athena Parthenos. This was accounted an impiety. He was imprisoned and died in prison, awaiting trial. Pheidias had previously been accused of appropriating gold that belonged to the great chryselephantine statue of Athena. Pericles had the gold taken from the statue and weighed, and so disproved the charge against his friend. The last great Periclean building, the Propylaea, Gate to the Acropolis, could not be completed, as Dörpfeld showed, according to the plan of the architect, Mnesicles, because of the ob-

32. Plut., *Pericles,* XXXII. See *Camb. Anc. Hist.* V, 384, 478, for the question of the date of the exiles of Protagoras and Anaxagoras.

33. Plut., *op. cit.*

34. Webster, *Sophocles, loc. cit.*

35. *O. T.,* 863 ff. The editors who find a political reference in this passage chiefly hold that it is directed against either Pericles or Alcibiades.

jections of priests of certain shrines, which stood in the
way of completion of the gate as planned. Although Pericles
himself appears to have professed *eusebeia*,[36] he was a thinking man and associated with thinkers. It is therefore not
improbable that the "impiety" of Pericles and his circle
may be assailed in verses *O. T.*, 863 ff., which speak about
the *hubris*[37] that breeds the tyrant and about his downfall. The verses, further, condemn the man who does not
reverence the statues of the gods, who seeks base gains,
and does not keep himself from impious deeds, but lays
his hands on holy things. We know of the great tension[38]
between Pericles' party and that of the anti-Periclean
priestly party in the last years of Pericles' life. It appears
likely that in these contests the sympathy of Sophocles would
be with the party of conservative religion. The lines are an
arraignment of irreligion far beyond that ascribed to Jocasta.

The heroine Antigone, daughter of Oedipus and (with
Ismene) "last root"[39] of the accursed house of Labdacus,
chooses to disobey the orders of Creon, who represents the
State,[40] and buries her brother, who fell in an attack on his
own city, Thebes. Thus she obeys the "Unwritten Laws,"
which ordain that burial should be given to all, rather than
the law of the State. Oedipus, father of Antigone, who,
though personally guiltless and a good man, was driven by
Apollo's oracle to kill his father and marry his mother, all
in ignorance, belonged to a legend which Aeschylus, Sophocles, and Euripides all dramatized. Sophocles is interested
in the drama of his fate, not in the explanation of the nature of the dealings of the gods with men.[41]

36. For the *eusebeia* of Pericles and his reverence for the Unwritten Laws,
see Thuc. II, 37; [Lys.] *Against Andocides*, 10.
37. Cf. Münzer, in *P. W. R. E.*, *XIX*, *s. v. Perikles*, cols. 774, 778, 779.
38. *Ibid.* Cf. Nestle, *op. cit.*, pp. 150 ff.
39. *Ant.*, 600.
40. Hegel, *Philosophie der Religion*, II, 133 f. (*Werke*, XII, Berlin, 1840),
discusses the play as a perfect example of conflict between two opposite right
principles—in this case family duty against allegiance due the state.
41. "Mit weltanschaulichen Fragen sollte man an den König Oedipus gar
nicht antreten." Schmid-Stählin, *op. cit.*, p. 371.

Two of the highest expressions of humanity in Sophocles
are made by two of his noblest characters, Antigone and
Oedipus. Antigone, in reply to Creon's statement that a
foe is never a friend, even in death, replies: "My nature
is to share love, not to share hatred."[42] This singularly beautiful and famous verse reveals the same spirit of loving kindness as that with which Oedipus' appeal to Tiresias ends.[43]
"For a man to help another with all his means and strength
is the noblest thing that man can do."

What Oedipus says here cannot be distorted, but the words
of Antigone, simple and clear as they are, have been twisted
by a recent writer[44] to mean something different from what
they say. He thinks that they should be translated as follows: "With the political strife of men I have nothing to
do; as a woman I have only to look after the claims of the
family." This is to take all beauty and feeling out of Antigone's wonderful words. To attain his meaning the writer
asserts that "love" on the lips of Ismene has a different
meaning from the sense in which Antigone uses it.[45] When
Ismene calls Antigone beloved,[46] she means she loves her;
when Antigone calls Polynices beloved,[47] she means he is a
member of the clan (Sippe). This quibbling is said by Weinstock[48] to be a characteristic of Sophocles. He cites, to support his contention, the disputed lines, Ant., 905 ff., in which
Antigone declares that had she been a mother of children
and a wife, she would never have defied the laws of the city
and buried her children, or her husband, since they could
have been replaced. In her brother's burial, she says, she
has defied the State because she can never have another
brother. Weinstock finds here the essential point of the whole
play; namely, that Antigone acts not from love, but from

42. *Ant.*, 523.
43. *O. T.*, 314 f.
44. Weinstock, *Sophokles*, p. 103.
45. *Ibid.*, 102 ff.
46. *Ant.*, 99; cf. 548.
47. *Ibid.*, 81.
48. Weinstock, *op. cit.*, pp. 103 f.

duty to blood-kinship, to those of the same tribe. She "loves" Polynices only because he is of her own blood. Weinstock does not consider the point that Antigone's children would have been of her blood and that therefore she would have had the duty of burying them. Robert,[49] who does weigh this argument, maintains that it is only from pride in race, because of the descent from her father's royal family, that Antigone buries her brother, whereas her children would have belonged to her husband's clan. Antigone, however, says about her duty to her brother, "it is right to show piety to those born of the same womb,"[50] thus including the mother as well as the father in the descent.

Antigone's speech, if genuine,[51] was probably inserted by Sophocles as a compliment to his friend Herodotus,[52] to whose history he makes frequent allusions in his plays. In this case the allusion is to the story of the wife of Intaphrenes, who, when offered by King Darius the choice of her husband's or her brother's life, chose that of her brother for the same reasons as those alleged by Antigone. It is a sophistical speech, which I think does not express Antigone's real character.

There can be no doubt that the "sympathy" of the poet was with the two great characters that he created in Antigone and Oedipus. Since Aristotle says that the disasters of the hero (or heroine) must come about through some error, there has been an extraordinary number of attempts to show some fault or guilt on the part of these two. Haste, a passionate temper, and stubbornness are the faults most frequently charged to them. The Chorus of old men in the *Antigone* say that she is fierce[53] and stubborn like her father.

49. Robert, *Oedipus*, pp. 332 ff.
50. *Ant.*, 511. Cf. Verrall, *Eumenides*, p. 120, n. on vv. 660–664, and Schmid-Stählin, *op. cit.*, p. 250 n. 1, for the question of Athenian opinion about descent from father and mother. Webster, *op. cit.*, p. 49.
51. It is considered an interpolation by many critics. Cf. Schmid-Stählin, *op. cit.*, p. 355 n. 2.
52. *Hdt.* III, 119.
53. *Ant.*, 471 f., 875.

A passionate temper is regarded as Oedipus' chief fault. But the curse of the house and the oracle were destined to work out in any case, even if father and daughter had been wholly characterless, and Antigone's desire to bury her brother and the desire of Oedipus to find out the cause of the plague which was devastating his city were not sins. I shall not discuss the endless question of the conflict between the right of the state,[54] represented by Creon, to forbid the burial of the dead enemy, and the right of the Unwritten Laws, by which Antigone is justified in burying that enemy because he is her brother. The interesting question is whether or not Sophocles had that "serenity" which is often attributed to him, when he contemplated the undeserved suffering of innocent people, and whether the thought of the inexorable laws (immanent in the curse, or the oracles), by which the innocent suffer, gave him an inner satisfaction, springing from his piety and acquiescence in the will of Heaven. With Aeschylus the sense of justice is so strong that he demands that Zeus should be just.[55] Euripides revolts against cruel gods and disbelieves tales of their wickedness. He belongs to the new movement of thought, the "Illumination," which produced the philosophical fourth century. Sophocles does not moralize[56] the gods, as Aeschylus did, nor reject them.

It is usually said that Sophocles goes back to the gods of Homer, but his gods do not resemble the light-hearted Homeric deities who can rejoice, sorrow, and be gay, like mortals. The gods in Sophocles are the representatives of the stern laws of Heaven. Their great attribute is power, and they are not touched by earthly troubles. It is strange that Sophocles was so little affected by the intellectual and moral ideas so freely discussed in the Periclean circle, in an

54. Cf. *inter alia*, Sikes, *op. cit.*, p. 51; Robert, *op. cit.*, pp. 342 ff.; Hegel, *loc. cit.*; A. C. Bradley, *Oxford Lectures on Poetry*, pp. 73 ff. "Hegel's Theory of Tragedy," London, 1934.

55. Cf. Prometheus' appeal to his Mother Earth and the Aether at the end of *P. V.* "Thou seest what injustice I suffer."

56. Cf. Schmid-Stählin, *op. cit.*, pp. 104, 465.

Athens that was beginning to be skeptical about ancestral curses and oracles, and desired, if it was to retain its gods, to moralize them. His dramas, very likely, would have suffered if he had allowed disbelief in the oracles to enter into them.

According to a recent authority[57] Sophocles has revealed to men the way to feel satisfied under the irresponsible rule of the Homeric gods. Sophocles is praised by this writer for simple and unquestioning faith in contrast to the skepticism and the desire to make the world better that appear in Euripides and in the *Prometheus Bound* of Aeschylus, which the author[58] whom I quote believes to have been written by an unknown poet, who was influenced by the sophists, and was on his way to Protagorean atheism.

The Unwritten Laws to which Antigone appeals[59] are the "high, heavenly laws," of which the Chorus in *Oedipus Tyrannus* sing in a famous passage. These laws are sometimes called κοινοὶ νόμοι, the universal laws of nature,[60] or the laws of the Greeks.[61] According to the discussion in the *Memorabilia*[62] they referred chiefly to man's duty to the gods and to parents, and to such crimes as murder and incest, and denying the rite of burial.

Antigone tells Creon that no human decree "could override the unwritten and secure laws of the gods, which are not of yesterday, but live forever, and no man knows when they were first made known." In the same tone the Chorus in *O. T.*, 863 ff., praise the laws of Heaven. The passage is often regarded as Sophocles' *credo*, the chorus being of the

57. *Ibid.*
58. W. Schmid, *Untersuchungen zum gefesselten Prometheus.* Stuttgart, 1929. Cf. G. Thomson, *op. cit.*, pp. 40 ff.
59. *Ant.*, 454 ff.
   Thuc. II, 37 (Pericles' Funeral Oration).
60. Aristotle, *Rhet.* I, 13, 2; Dem. XVIII, 275.
61. Euripides, *Heraclidae*, 1010 f.
62. Xenophon, *Mem.* 4, 4, 19. Cf. E. Bruhn, *König Oedipus*, Berlin, 1910, n. on 865 ff., "die Gebote welche auf der Sitte beruhten" were called ἄγραφοι (unwritten) even when they were collected and catalogued, which appears to have been done early. (Aesch., *Suppl.* 693: Euripides, *Heraclidae, Frag.* 853.)

nature of a *parabasis*,[63] or personal expression of opinion on the part of the poet.

The occasion of the passage, it is often said, is the "blasphemy" of Jocasta, who, under great stress, has said that she no longer believes in divination. Some think that, though the Chorus still believe in him, Oedipus is also glanced at because he acquiesced[64] in his wife's words. It is unreasonable and, in my judgment, impossible to see references to Jocasta in the obscure denunciations of tyrants and those who have no reverence for the statues[65] of the gods, and do not refrain from unjust gains, but lay their hands on sacred objects. It seems clear that there is some contemporary reference here, perhaps to the charges against Pericles and Pheidias, 432–430 B.C., and members of Pericles' circle, or to the profane acts of which Alcibiades was accused in 415 B.C., in connection with the desecration of the Mysteries and the mutilation of the Hermae. Either crisis would be a possible occasion for this outburst against destroyers of holy things and both occasions have had their advocates. Verses 896–910 definitely refer to prevailing disbelief in the oracles, and are probably pointed at Jocasta, as well as at Athenian skepticism.

It is the first strophe that was so much admired by Matthew Arnold and I give his translation.

"Oh! that my lot may lead me in the path of holy innocence of word and deed, the path which august laws ordain, laws that in the highest empyrean had their birth, neither did the race of mortal men beget them, nor shall oblivion ever put them to sleep. The power of God is mighty in them, and groweth not old."

It is a noble passage, but I think that Matthew Arnold has read into it an ethical spirit that the Greek does not

63. Schmid-Stählin, *op. cit.*, pp. 105, 370, 485.
64. "Thou judgest well." *O. T.*, 859.
65. Cf. Jebb on *O. T.*, 886.

justify. The words which he translates "holy innocence"[66] refer to ritual purity, strict observance of religious duties.[67] The laws "begotten in the empyrean" are the primitive old laws which early Greek society had evolved.

The song praises ritual guiltlessness and prophesies woe for the irreligious and the unbeliever. It is difficult even for those who consider Jocasta a godless fiend and Oedipus a sinner and a blasphemer to make the burden of it apply to them. There is so much in it that does not fit them. Those who heard the chorus first, whether in 428 B.C.[68] after the disgrace of Pericles' friends, or in 415 B.C.[69] after the irreligious acts of which Alcibiades was accused, could interpret the whole as we cannot, but assuredly to them its "religious sentiment" would mean something more limited in scope than what his translation of part of it meant to the nineteenth-century Matthew Arnold. At least the Heavenly Laws which inspired what he said about the religion of Sophocles were to him something more deeply moralized than the Unwritten Laws to which Antigone appealed for her sanction in burying her brother, and the Laws, by ignorantly transgressing which Jocasta was driven to suicide and Oedipus to a misery worse than death. These laws were[70] old taboos,[71] social sanctions, which were attributed to the gods and marked the limit of ethics which the traditional folk-morality had reached.

I have dwelt on these two passages about the Unwritten and the Heavenly Laws, because they are constantly quoted to show that Sophocles believed in "an immutable moral

66. The Greek words mean freedom from ritual guilt, blood guiltiness etc. Cf. Eur., *Heraclidae*, 1011. "My death will bring the curse of bloodguilt on my slayer."

67. Nestle, *op. cit.*, pp. 132 f.

68. Cf. Jebb. *O. T.*, 30 and *ad loc.* Cambridge, 1902.

69. Cf. Dindorf, *O. T.*, 1, 873 (note). Oxford, 1860.

70. Cf. Nestle, *op. cit.*, p. 132. They are "Braüche der herrschenden Religion"; i.e., customs rather than conscience.

71. Xen., *Mem.*, 4, 4, 19. Myres, *Political Ideas of the Greeks*, pp. 282 ff. Thalheim, *P. W.*, I, 898.

order or law,"[72] "the Law of God." Such expressions used about his belief suggest a much more moralized and modern standpoint than is warranted by what is found in Greek authors about these laws. They represent, as I have said, old social customs which had become binding and religious, involving a curse if transgressed. They were few in number[73] and ordained burial of the dead, not merely kindred dead, *(Ajax, Antigone, Suppliant Women* of Euripides), punishment for murder of kindred *(Eumenides, Oedipus Tyrannus),* forbade incest *(Oedipus Tyrannus),* and commanded honoring of the gods, and honoring parents *(Oedipus at Colonus).*[74] Plato calls them "ancient customs and usages." "However the city performs sacrifice, the ancient law (custom) is best."[75] From the evidence offered by the extant plays, Sophocles, who was a priest of the health divinity, Amynos,[76] and was himself worshiped after his death under the title Dexion, clung in a changing world to the worship of the old gods and the old religion.[77] He ranks *eusebeia,* piety, as the first of the virtues. Seven years after the death of Sophocles Athens killed Socrates on a charge of *asebeia,* impiety. The Athenians had not yet learned the lessons that Socrates and Euripides had taught, and they believed that they served the gods and their state by banishing the one and killing the other.

Together with *eusebeia* is coupled *aidos* (which takes its color from the connection in which it is used) in that play of terrible vengeance, the *Electra.* "If the dead man shall lie[78] wrapped in earth and nothingness, and they (his mur-

72. J. Adams, *The Religious Teachers of Greece,* pp. 165 ff. Edinburgh, 1908.

73. Myres, *loc. cit.* Bruhn, *op. cit.,* n. on v. 865 ff. Nestle, *loc. cit.*

74. Cf. *O. C.,* 1382. Cf. 1361 ff., 1377. Plato, Laws, 793.

75. Hesiod, *Frag.* 20 (Evelyn-White, p. 728).

76. Or Alkon. Cf. Kern, *op. cit.,* II, 313 f., 314 n. 1.

77. Nestle, *op. cit.,* "Thyestes according to an oracle must (in the Sophoclean play *Thyestes*) beget a child by his own daughter, Pelopia, to avenge him on his brother Atreus—his religious sanction."

78. *El.,* 250.

derers) shall not pay the penalty of blood for blood, then reverence and the piety of all mortals will vanish away." Electra says this. Later she tells her sister[79] that if she will join her in slaying their mother and Aegisthus, she will get credit for piety from their dead father in the world below and from their brother, whom they believe to be dead.

The keynote of this great, but least-loved play of Sophocles is the piety of vengeance.[80] Electra's joy in the murder of her mother seems to most readers fiendish, but she is praised by certain writers because "she executes the will of God." Sophocles "does not consider the right or wrong of her deed. Since God commanded it, it is right."[81]

Many circumstances unknown to us may have impelled Sophocles to write this play, which demands "burning for burning, wound for wound, stripe for stripe." He was a genius, but an aging one. Fundamental ideas about the vengeance of the gods were not likely to change in a man over eighty years old,[82] and the events of the Peloponnesian War and its evil effects on Greek character may have confirmed him in his belief in the Ancient Laws. His Antigone is lovable, although critics like Robert and Weinstock attempt to take from her all human qualities, leaving her only a barren *eusebeia*. Electra is in type an exaggeration of the character of Antigone. In spite of the sympathy that is aroused by the depiction of her sufferings at the hands of Clytemnestra and Aegisthus the general feeling is that she is the least noble of the Sophoclean heroines. Her vengeful *eusebeia* is not like the love (*pace* some German critics) which actuated Antigone, and the "happy ending," when all

79. *Ibid.*, 968. Cf. 1096, where Electra is praised for her piety toward Zeus.

80. In this play and in the *Thyestes* of Sophocles there is a conflict between the oracle of Apollo and the Unwritten Laws concerning blood-guiltiness (*Electra*) and incest (*Thyestes*). For the plot of the *Thyestes* see Robert, *Die Griechische Heldensage*, pp. 298 ff.

81. Weinstock, *op. cit.*, p. 33. Cf. pp. 34–39.

82. I agree with Schmid-Stählin's dating of the *Electra* of Sophocles in 415 B.C., *op. cit.*, p. 389.

the misery to come is known to the audience, produces a strange impression.

The Sophoclean Electra has been explained as follows. "She is a normal woman, changed by circumstances and a *bad creed* [italics mine] to the wretch who bids her brother 'Strike again, if you have strength,' although the victim is her mother."[83] According to most interpreters of the Sophoclean play[84] that "bad creed" was the *eusebeia* not only of Electra, but also of Sophocles, the *eusebeia* that is hymned in *O. T.*, 863 ff., the creed of the Ancient Heavenly Laws.

Although the virtue *eusebeia* in the plays of Sophocles is ritual, severe, and inexorable when transgressed, the great humane virtues live in and distinguish his characters more fully than in any others in Greek literature except those of Homer. It is in them that the real Sophocles exists, not in the narrow *eusebeia* which, however, forms an effective tragic background for his plays and makes them in reality tragedies of fate. And, as Professor Murray says,[85] we have no right to suppose that Sophocles thought of the moral questions raised in his plays exactly as the people in the plays do. Even the Chorus does not always express his views.[86]

The *Ajax*, after the clash between divinity, sensitive to any human defiance of its power and claims, and the simple-minded, boastful hero, proud of his physical strength and valor, presents wonderful examples of love, in the "bride won by the spear,"[87] the captive, Tecmessa, loveliest of Sophoclean heroines, in the Chorus of sailors, who are devoted to their chief and in the brother, Teucer. Odysseus, from the beginning of the play, in his dialogue with Athena, shows humanity in high degree. After Athena has pointed

---

83. Sheppard, *Camb. Anc. History*, V, 130.

84. Cf. Weinstock, *op. cit.*, pp. 259 ff. *et pass.*

85. *Oedipus* (translation), p. vi.

86. For criticism of the cruelty of the gods, see *Trach.*, 1266 ff., and *Philoctetes*, 446 ff.

87. *Ajax*, 146, 894. Cf. Briseis, her forerunner, who was also "won by the spear." *Il.* IX, 343.

out to him the power of the gods, who have changed a man
so eminently prudent and valiant into a raving maniac,[88]
Odysseus replies, "I pity him in his misery, although he is
my enemy. He is yoked to a bitter doom. I look at my own
life as well as his, for I see that we who live are but phan-
toms and empty shadows."

Athena's reply to this stresses the lesson of humility before the gods, a faint reflection of the old doctrine of the
jealousy of the gods. She also remarks that the gods love the
self-controlled and hate bad men. With that she or, rather,
her voice—for she is not visible—disappears. In the second
half of the play, after the suicide of Ajax, Odysseus shows
the same fine spirit in opposing the brutality of Menelaus
and Agamemnon, who refuse the rites of burial for Ajax.
Odysseus does not appeal to the laws of the gods alone, although he refers to them. After saying that he would never
treat Ajax, though his enemy, with dishonor, he says to
Agamemnon,

"It is not just that he should be dishonored by you. You
would not hurt him, but the laws of the gods. It is not right
to injure the good man when he dies, not even if you chance
to hate him."

Agamemnon, after remarking that it is hard for a king
to show piety, yields to Odysseus, though he still declares
that he has in his heart undying hatred for Ajax. Odysseus
tells Teucer that he is ready to be the friend of Ajax, as
he has been his foe, and that he would be glad to join in his
burial rites. Teucer refuses to allow this participation, fear-
ing that it might offend his brother's spirit. He thanks Odysseus and praises his nobility. So the play ends with the victory of the humane spirit (*aidos*) over the inhumanity and irreligion of the two Atreidae.

88. Rohde, *Psyche,* translated from the eighth edition by W. B. Hillis, p.
428. London and New York, 1925—"divine inhumanity and cold lust of vengeance manifest themselves—clearly—in the Athene of the *Ajax.*"

The influence of Euripides[89] appears in the two romantic plays, the *Trachinian Women* and the *Philoctetes*. In these the heroine Deianeira and the hero Philoctetes are innocent sufferers, and the plot is treated from the point of view of dramatic interest, rather than that of ancestral sin, vengeance of the gods, and the Unwritten Laws.

The ethical quality of the *Philoctetes* completely satisfies the moral sense. The young Neoptolemus has both *aidos* and *eleos*,[90] pity for the suffering Philoctetes and shame for the part he himself has played in deceiving the hero in order to rob him of his bow, on which the fate of Troy depends. His decision to do the right thing at the sacrifice of all his ambitions reminds us of his father's renunciation of his terrible vengeance on Hector.

In all of his plays, except in the evil and morbid atmosphere of his *Electra,* the poet makes us feel the greatness of the human spirit and the splendor of humanity.

"Many are wonderful things, but none more wonderful than Man," is the song of his chorus in the *Antigone*. And now that his gods have vanished and his Ancient Laws are interpreted in a humane and scientific spirit rather than in that of ritual *eusebeia,* the nobility of the characters which he created remains untouched by time. His gods were relentless and inhuman. His men and women were moved by *aidos* and *sophrosyne* and by pity. They are great and noble figures, and their suffering makes the Sophoclean tragedy.

89. G. H. Macurdy, *Classical Review*, XXV (1911), 97 ff.; "The Chronology of the Extant Plays of Euripides," pp. 63 ff. Schmid-Stählin, *op. cit.,* pp. 374 f., 378, 383, 398 f., 397 ff.

T. v. Wilamowitz-Moellendorff, *Die Dramatische Technik des Sophokles,* pp. 273 f. Berlin, 1917.

90. Cf. *Il.,* XXIV, 44.

XI

HUMANITY IN EURIPIDES

THE POET OF THE ENLIGHTENMENT[1]

EURIPIDES died in Macedon in 407 B.C. The old Sophocles[2] put on black garments to show his grief, and led his actors and chorus ungarlanded into the Odeion for their rehearsal. They had been rivals in the theatre and had written, each in his own way, on the same themes, but there had not been hatred between them, although Sophocles held to the old *eusebeia*, the old legends, and the sanctity of the Unwritten Laws, while Euripides had his face turned toward the future, thought, and taught his audiences to think and to question old immoralities, and injustices in the traditional religion.[4] He keeps to the outlines of the old myths, but makes significant changes[5] in details, approaching so closely to everyday life in his treatment of character that he is the destroyer of the heroic tragedy and the creator of the drama of the fourth century and of the modern theatre.

Three men, Euripides, Socrates, and Thucydides,[6] stand out as splendid representatives of the age of Enlightenment in Athens and as shapers of the intellectual life and thought that were to come. Socrates is in love, he says,[7] with philosophy. His interest is the soul of man and virtue; Thucydides is in love with the objective and scientific truth of history, and Euripides with humanity. The monument of Socrates is the philosophy of Plato, set forth in those *Dialogues* in

1. W. Nestle, *Der Dichter der griechischen Aufklärung.* Stuttgart, 1901.
2. *Vita,* 44.
3. Euripides reverences these laws also. Cf. *Heraclidae,* 110, *Supplices,* 311, 526 ff. *Fragment of Heraclidae,* 853.
4. Aristophanes, *Frogs,* 1009.
5. Pindar, Aeschylus, and Sophocles also make changes in the myths.
6. According to one tradition Thucydides wrote the epitaph of Euripides.
7. Plato, *Gorgias,* 481 D.

which Socrates still lives and teaches; that of Thucydides is
his magnificent and imperishable[8] contribution to political
history; Euripides has his monument in his extant work in
tragedy, and the influence that the spirit of his dramas had
on the intellectual and moral thought of the world.

These men and those who shared their rationalistic views
were regarded by the conservatives in Athens as dangerous
intellectuals, and for this reputation one of them paid the
death penalty and another was, apparently more than once,
prosecuted for impiety. Thucydides wrote[9] his history in an
exile that was not the result of his opinions, but of an alleged
military blunder.

Persecution for opinions about questions of morality and
religion has been a frequent phenomenon in history, and
now that thought and mercy are forbidden in countries which
have been centres of light and learning, it is the easier to
understand why, even in the time of Enlightenment in
Athens, the poet who hated cruelty and said that pity could
not live among the ignorant was finally obliged to leave
a city which, after long years of war, was forgetting what
pity and what wisdom meant.

The sophists had taught Athens to argue and to reason;
some of them had taught the young ambitious men how in
their speeches in the assembly and the law courts to make
the worse case look the better. This charge was brought
against Socrates. We know that it was not justified, and that
it was the truth that he sought. Euripides can make his
characters argue like sophists; his spirit, however, was not
sophistic, but truth-seeking. Dieterich,[10] in no unflattering
sense, says of him, "he was the greatest sophist of them all;
the one who contributed most to spread the conception of
the new world and to destroy the old way of looking at the

8. Thuc. I, 22 (the last sentence).
9. Cf. J. H. Finley, Jr., "Euripides and Thucydides," *Harvard Studies,*
XLIX (1938), pp. 64 ff., for the influence of the intellectual life of Periclean
Athens on the *History* of Thucydides.
10. *P. W.,* VI, col. 1279.

world *(Weltanschauung)*. His revolutionary preaching in its effect and its power goes endlessly far beyond all that Protagoras and the other sophists had attained."

Sophocles has been praised by Matthew Arnold in a well-known poem, on the ground that he "saw life steadily and saw it whole." He has often been eulogized for his lack of sentimentality and his cheerful religion. Gilbert Murray[11] has called our attention to A. W. von Schlegel's commendation of the gaiety *(himmlische Heiterkeit)* with which the murder of Clytemnestra is performed by her two children. Schlegel[12] admires the "fresh breath of life and youth that blows through the whole action." Naturally, he finds the Electra of Euripides guilty of "most shameful repentance after the murder, a repentance that is not a moral feeling, but an animal revulsion." He objects also to the "blasphemies" against the Delphic oracle, which, as Schlegel believes, destroy the whole drama. "What possessed Euripides," he asks, "to measure himself with Aeschylus and Sophocles, and to write an *Electra*"? This question has been repeated by many scholars, who follow Schlegel in his belief that it was an impudence in Euripides to bring his *Electra* before a public that had seen the Sophoclean *Electra* produced on the stage.[13]

Gilbert Murray holds to the older belief of Wilamowitz[14] in the priority of the Euripidean *Electra*. He has, however, seen the true reason for the Euripidean play; namely, that to Euripides "the mother-murder, like most acts of revenge, but more than most—was a sin and a horror."[15] And he has also shown that it is a thoughtless and shallow judgment that

11. *Electra of Euripides,* p. vi. Cf. also F. A. Paley, Euripides, II, 319, 322.
12. A. W. von Schlegel, *Vorlesungen über dramatische Kunst und Litteratur,* pp. 161 ff. Leipzig, 1846.
13. For a partial list of scholars who assail the Euripidean *Electra* and its author, see *Philologus* CVI (1897), pp. 562 ff.
14. Wilamowitz renounced this belief in *Hermes,* XXXIV (1899), p. 57 n. 2.
15. *Electra of Euripides,* p. VII.

calls Electra in Euripides a corrupt and evil character,[16] a judgment often uttered by those who see in the heroine of the other dramatist a noble and pious woman.

One English voice before that of Gilbert Murray was raised in defense of the *Electra* of Euripides, that of F. A. Paley,[17] who protested against the attacks on the play and on Euripides made "by those to whom Greek mythology is a more interesting subject than the human passions." The German critics, from Schlegel to Wilamowitz and to those of the present time,[18] have glorified the Sophoclean play and condemned the Euripidean, and much English criticism has been influenced by the German point of view.

But a satisfactory answer to the question, "Why did Euripides write his Electra?" has been given by Steiger.[19] Euripides wrote the play in moral indignation against the spirit of Sophocles' *Electra,* with its cruel conception of Apollo, and its glorification of the impious deed of mother murder, which Sophocles had represented as a pious act. "Not only is Sophocles attacked, but Apollo, the entire heroic age, and the belief in the personages that still appeared on the stage." "Morally it was better to doubt with Euripides than to believe with Sophocles."[20] (Those "who believed with Sophocles" put Socrates to death.) Steiger observes that, as a contemporary and rival playwright, Euripides would not regard the work of Sophocles with such awe as is often felt toward it by modern scholars. He was himself a man of genius, with a searching philosophical mind and a great interest in the problems of life. Sophocles was no speculative thinker. Wilamowitz compares his religious belief with that of a pious little old woman (*Mütterlein*) of the present

16. Cf. G. Kaibel, *Sophokles Elektra,* p. 56. Electra of Euripides utterly corrupt, her repentance nervous tension, the heroine herself a repulsive specimen of humanity, etc.

17. *Euripides,* II, 319 ff.

18. Cf. Weinstock, *op. cit.,* pp. 11–39.

19. *Philologus,* CVI (1897), "Warum schrieb Euripides seine Electra?" pp. 561 ff.

20. *Op. cit.,* p. 600.

day, who sees the hand of a personal, righteous God in all the unintelligible and undeserved sorrows of her life.

It is always said that Sophocles, the "idealist," goes back to the Heroic Age in religious sentiment and that he represents characters of heroic stature, "as they[21] should be" as he himself said. Euripides, looking at the life about him, pictures men and women, in Sophocles' words "as they really are." In view of this, one may ask just what Matthew Arnold's famous line about Sophocles means and how far it is consistent with the facts. It appears to have been Euripides who looked at life.

It is true that while Euripides is a realist so far as the inherited tradition of the Greek stage and theatre would permit, the two poets reacted on and against one another. Sophocles has realistic "Euripidean" characters such as Deianeira, and the plays of Euripides represent heroic girls who sacrifice themselves for country or for husband and children, like Antigone in her sacrifice of life and happiness for her brother's sake. If we had more of their two hundred and more plays, we should doubtless see more of this mutual influence in theme and treatment.

I have referred particularly to the two *Electras* because in them the fundamental opposition of the two poets in their feeling about the oracles and humanity is most strikingly apparent. From the point of view of "modern" and moralized thought the *Electra* of Euripides is immeasurably higher in religious and ethical feeling.[22] Euripides as a thinking man in that period of Enlightenment could not but be skeptical about the Delphic oracle. In this he was in advance of Sophocles, who was "a being of instinct rather than of thought, a mystic as much as a realist."[23] It is a curious anomaly that

---

21. Aristotle, *Poetics*, 1460b.

22. Steiger, *op. cit.*, pp. 564, 592 ff. Steiger points out that Euripides regarded it as his sacred duty to go in advance of his people in the path to higher morality, and to raise them above the primitive moral views of the Heroic Age. See also Nestle, *op. cit.*, p. 368. "His age has misunderstood him; the afterworld has appreciated him; history has justified him."

23. R. W. Livingstone, *Greek Poetry and Life*, p. 163. Oxford, 1936.

Schlegel[24] and others are so indignant at Euripidean "blasphemies" against the Delphic oracle and commend Sophocles for his belief in them, though they themselves have no belief at all in Apollo.

The *Electra* of Sophocles ends with a burst of joy from the chorus,

> O seed of Atreus, after many sufferings
> you have come forth in freedom,
> made perfect by this deed.

All is happiness, and, as Schlegel says, "gaiety." An admirer of the play, who sees it closing with an act of divine justice, says,

"Yet the mother-murder so lightly taken remains always a weak spot in this drama."[25]

At the close of Euripides' *Electra* Castor and Polydeuces, brothers of Clytemnestra, appear in the air as *dei ex machina,* coming between two merciful errands of convoying ships at sea and helping mariners. Castor chides Apollo for the oracle that caused the crime of matricide. This is a typical piece of Euripidean "blasphemy."[26]

> Our sister's death was just, unjust your deed.
> 'Twas Phoebus, Phoebus!—still, he is our lord,
> So much I say—though wise, he gave to you
> An oracle not wise; this you must bear.

There is another play in which I believe Euripides is replying to the ideas of Sophocles and is upholding a view of life that is more humane than the conservatively religious view of the older poet. This play is the *Mad Heracles.* The act of Hera in driving the hero insane is reminiscent of the part played by Athena in the *Ajax,* but it is the moral of the *Oedipus* which I think Euripides is opposing.

---

24. *Op. cit.,* I, 139, 161. Cf. Wilamowitz, *Hermes,* XVIII (1883), 233.
25. Bernhardy, *Grundriss der Griechischen Litteratur,* II, 349. Halle, 1877.
26. He attacks the god still more strongly in the previous plays, *Andromache* (417), *Ion* (416), *I. T.* (414). These are my datings. See *Chronology,* pp. 38 ff. The strongest expressions of disbelief occur in the fragments of the *Bellerophon.*

In the *Mad Heracles*,[27] the hero returns to Thebes after completing his labors and slays the brutal tyrant Lycus. The first half of the play shows Megara, Heracles' wife, and her little children, threatened with death by the usurping tyrant, who wishes to destroy the young heirs to the throne. After the slaying of Lycus by Heracles the Chorus in a joyful song praise the gods for this display of their power.

The goddess Hera then displays *her* power by sending the spirit of Madness in bodily form to drive Heracles into a fit of insanity, in which he kills his children and his wife. The "happy ending" of the first part of the play (up to v. 816, where the Chorus first see Lussa, the spirit of Madness, descending) forms an ironic contrast to the second part, in which Heracles is driven mad, recovers his sanity, and is discovered in his awful plight by Theseus who has come from Athens with troops to depose the tyrant Lycus, of whose death he has not heard. The significance of the play lies in the scene between Heracles and Theseus. Heracles, an innocent sinner like Oedipus, has, like that hero, contracted the stain of pollution.[28] Theseus, who speaks like an Athenian of the time of Enlightenment, tells his friend Heracles to uncover his head, which he has covered for fear of polluting the sun, for Theseus says:[29] "No mortal can pollute the gods." This is against the conventional belief at Athens and against the view of Sophocles, expressed in *O. T.*, 1224–1227. Theseus also has no fear of contracting a ritual pollution from the sight or touch[30] of this morally guiltless slayer. Heracles has thought of suicide, but Theseus shows

---

27. Cf. Livingstone, *op. cit.*, p. 160.

28. *H. F.*, 1155.

29. *Ibid.*, 1232.

Cf. *Antigone,* 1043 and Webster, *op. cit.*, p. 52, for Sophocles' belief in the opposite theory.

30. Cf. *H. F.*, 1155 f., 1162, 1219, 1232 ff.

Weinstock, *op. cit.*, p. 294, believes that *v.* 1232 of the *Heracles* is answered by Sophocles in the *Antigone* (cf. Weinstock, pp. 189 f.). This opinion ignores the date of the *Heracles*. Weinstock's criticism of the "heresy" of Euripides is interesting and revealing.

him a better way; namely, to go with him to Athens and be cleansed from his ritual stain, and then dwell in that city, sharing wealth and honor with Theseus. "For it will be a splendid crown for my city to obtain from Greece the fame and glory of helping a good man."

The two heroes, Oedipus and Heracles, sin in ignorance and neither is morally guilty. Oedipus has sinned against the Unwritten Laws and (slightly) against the oracle of Apollo. Heracles has killed his wife and children unknowingly, because of the spite of Hera, on whom the real guilt is squarely laid by the Chorus,[31] by Amphitryo,[32] by Theseus,[33] and by Heracles.[34] There is no song in praise of her to match the chorus[35] in praise of the Heavenly Laws and the oracles, by which Oedipus perished. Moreover, in order to hearten Heracles, Theseus mentions all sorts of evil deeds committed with impunity by the gods, who feel no pangs at all at having sinned. Heracles, suddenly a child of the Enlightenment, says that he does not believe these bad old stories. They are shameful legends told by the bards.[36] Paley's comment on this is very illuminating. He says: "For these and like sentiments, often fearlessly expressed, unthinking men in ancient as well as in modern times called Euripides an infidel. He was not sure of the true nature of God; but he was sure that if such a being existed at all, he must be very different from that which the fables of poets represented him to be."[37]

After saying that God, if He exists, needs no material thing, Heracles declares that he will not be a coward, for a

31. 1311 f.
32. 1127.
33. 1191.
34. 1264 ff., 1303–1310.
35. *O. T.*, 863 ff.
36. *H. F.*, 1346.

37. Cf. Nestle, *op. cit.*, p. 136. "The crucial reason for Euripides' disbelief in the folk-religion is not polytheism, but the immorality of the gods. Sophocles infers that the gods must be good even if they bid one leave the path of right."

brave man must endure what is fated for him to bear. He will go with Theseus to Athens.

I believe that in dramatizing the fate of Heracles, an innocent hero persecuted by Hera, and driven by her to awful deeds, Euripides had in mind the Sophoclean Oedipus, also innocent, but, because of the oracle, committing horrible sins in ignorance. Since Sophocles thinks that Oedipus, though innocent, must suffer, Euripides has Theseus explain to Heracles that his guilt is purely ritual and that there is no pollution incurred in the sight or touch of him. Oedipus blinds himself. Heracles is induced by his friend to agree to come with him to Athens, where, after he has been purified ritually from the stain of bloodshed, he shall have an abiding-place and after his death shall be honored with a shrine, where the city shall worship him.[38] The play was written, I believe, by Euripides, as an answer to the *Oedipus,* in which, instead of eulogy of the heavenly powers that pursue mankind with undeserved suffering, Hera's persecution of Heracles is bitterly condemned. "Who could pray to such a goddess,[39] who through jealousy of Zeus, ruined the man who served all Hellas well and did no wrong?" Heracles is "the glorious Heracles,"[40] as Oedipus is "the glorious Oedipus,"[41] and both are saviors of their lands. Besides the arraignment of the legend about the gods and the expression of disbelief in them and in pollution[42] caused by seeing or touching a man who had shed blood, however innocently, Euripides also demonstrates that the undeserved evil that comes upon a good man does not necessarily crush him, that a strong man like Heracles can be saved from self-destruction by the help of a friend like Theseus. The last words of

38. Cf. the so-called *Theseum,* on the metopes of which the deeds of Theseus and of Heracles are sculptured.

39. *H. F.,* 1308 ff.

40. *Ibid.,* 1414.

41. *O. T.,* 8.

42. Cf. *I. T.,* 380 ff., where this belief is scoffed at by Iphigenia. These ideas are called "stupidity," in *I. T.,* 386. Cf. *H. F.,* 1254. Cf. Weinstock, *loc. cit.,* for discussion of Sophocles' belief in "pollution."

Heracles, almost the last words of the play, are: "He who sets wealth or strength above good friends is mad." The drama closes on the note of friendship. The Chorus leaves the stage singing, "We go in sorrow and in bitter grief, having lost the very noblest of our friends."

It is a great and humane play. Browning, who translated it, called it "the perfect piece." Yet it is not always well thought of, even now. Norwood,[43] for example, says: "But to be blunt, what is the play about?" The apparent lack of unity between the two parts of the play disturbs some critics. As I have said, the first part serves as a background for the second.

In this play, as strongly as in any, Euripides condemns the "shameful legends of the bards" about the gods and attempts to substitute a purer theology.[44] If the gods conform to human immorality, why should they not conform to human morality?

We are fortunate in having such a noble document, which shows the child of the Enlightenment in Athens in the very struggle and travail of thought, endeavoring to present to his audiences the new morality that was invading religion. What Heracles says about disbelief in the immorality of the gods and their quarrels for supremacy goes back to Xenophanes of Colophon,[45] who in the sixth century B.C. reproached Homer and Hesiod for their anthropomorphic stories about the gods, denied divination, and said that God was One.

There are in the other plays of Euripides many interesting passages of protest against the prevailing religious ideas,

---

43. G. Norwood, *Greek Tragedy*, p. 229, London, 1920 (Norwood seems to incline toward accepting Verrall's elaborate theory that the motive of the play is to suggest the falsity of the traditional stories about Heracles.) Cf. Wilamowitz, *Euripides Herakles*, I, 132. Berlin, 1895, "es ist ein selbstbekenntnis des Euripides, es ist sein ἐγκαρτερήσω βίοτον." *Ibid.*, p. 130, "ich trag' es dennoch."

44. *H. F.*, 1314 ff., 1340 ff. Cf. Plato, *Republic*, 382 D. "There is no lying poet in God."

45. *Frags.*, 1, 11, 14, 15, 16, 34. Cf. Euripides, *H. F.*, 1315 ff. and 1340 ff.

and expressions of his own philosophical idea of God. I will cite but one, the most famous, from the *Trojan Women*.[46]

> Thou deep Base of the World, and thou high Throne
> Above the world, whoe'er thou art, unknown
> And hard of surmise, Chain of Things to be,
> Or Reason of our Reason;[47] God[48] to thee
> I lift my praise, seeing the silent road
> That bringeth justice ere the end be trod.
> To all that breathes and dies.

To this extraordinary prayer I should give the praise that Matthew Arnold gives to the famous chorus about the Heavenly Laws[49] in Sophocles. It has been often said that we must not look to Sophocles for moralization of myths or for speculations about the world and man.[50] Euripides could not keep from such thinking, and being a professional dramatist, highly gifted as a tragic poet, he found in the stage a means for combining drama and moral teaching.[51]

Those who are interested in the history of thought owe a debt of gratitude to two interpreters of the Euripidean drama, Professor Gilbert Murray[52] and F. L. Lucas.[53] Their work stands out from the monotonous mass of those who have so little understanding of the poet and so little imagination that they have called him an infidel [sic], a hater of women, a corrupter of morals, etc. Lucas, after citing Goethe's expressions of contempt for Schlegel's opinion and that of the philologists, "who cavil at Euripides because he has so long been cavilled at," says very truly that "the admired of Milton and Goethe can afford a few hundred Schlegels and La Harpes."

Professor Murray and Mr. Lucas have shown, with in-

46. 884–888. Gilbert Murray's translation.
47. Literally "whether the Necessity of Nature or the Mind of Man."
48. Zeus.
49. *O. T.*, 863 ff.
50. Cf. Schmid-Stählin, *op. cit.*, pp. 371, 465, *et pass.*
51. Aristophanes, *Frogs, loc. cit.*
52. *Euripides and His Age* (1913).
53. *Euripides* (1923).

sight and with knowledge of the dramatist and the epoch in which he lived, the high quality of Euripides' genius and character, his exquisite sensibility, his pity for the oppressed and bitter hatred of cruelty and the oppressor, and his "fearless freedom of thought."[54]

"The most tragic of the poets" calls forth pity, as in their extant plays Aeschylus and Sophocles do not, by putting on the stage small children, whose terror and grief bring out in relief the barbarity of some tyrant, such as Lycus in the *Mad Heracles* and Menelaus in the *Andromache*. Sophocles had brought the child of Ajax on the stage to receive his father's farewell and blessing, but in Euripides the child sometimes speaks and expresses his grief or terror. Eumelus in the *Alcestis,* one of the two children of the heroine, is present when she dies, and pleads with her not to leave them. Andromache's little son by Neoptolemus, Molossus, has a part in the terrified dialogue[55] with his mother, when Menelaus is threatening to kill them. In this scene a metaphor much loved by Euripides appears—that of the mother bird covering her young with her wings. Molossus says, "O Mother, Mother! I creep beneath your wing." Eumelus in the *Alcestis* calls himself his mother's nestling, and Megara in the *Mad Heracles,* threatened by Lycus, says: "I try to save my little ones, gathering them under my wings as a bird her nestlings."[56]

The theme of mother love pervades the tragedy of the savage Medea, who loves,[57] yet slays her children. Most pitiful of all is the anguish of Andromache over the fate of her son by Hector, the child Astyanax, in the *Trojan Women*. Here Euripides has made a heartrending picture of the sacrifice of the child in the horror of warfare. No one had ever represented the baseness of war before this wonderful

54. Lucas, *op. cit.,* pp. 34, 38, "Courage was his and pity."
55. *Andromache,* 505–544.
56. Cf. for the same metaphor, *Heraclidae,* 10. (The old Iolaus speaks.)
57. Cf. *Medea,* 1040 ff.

drama, which Haigh has unimaginatively called "the least interesting of the extant tragedies."[58]

A countless number of little Astyanaxes have been killed but lately and are still being slaughtered for the glory of the war lords and their undying shame. I quote from Gilbert Murray's often-quoted and noble preface to his translation. "The *Troades* itself has indeed almost no fierceness and singularly little thought of revenge. It is only the crying of one of the great wrongs of the world wrought into music as it were, and made beautiful by 'the most tragic of the poets.' "

I have considered the plays of Euripides, the *Electra* and the *Mad Heracles,* as humanistic replies to two plays of Sophocles which do not depart from the traditional beliefs. Dieterich[59] notes that while the two poets learned from one another throughout their lives, it is not difficult to discern in Euripides veiled polemic against Sophocles. In my opinion the polemic is not veiled but obvious in these two plays, the "moral" or underlying motive of which is directed against the tradition upheld by Sophocles.

The studies of the characters of women, for which Euripides was famous, begin for us with the beautiful *Alcestis* of 438 B.C. The two poets both contended at this dramatic festival, Sophocles receiving the first prize and Euripides the second. The three other plays presented by Euripides are lost, as well as those presented by Sophocles. The *Alcestis,* with its happy ending, took the place of a satyr drama, which usually was the last of the set of four plays.

Alcestis is one of the most beautiful heroines in tragedy. In her case there is no question, such as is often raised about Antigone's motive. Alcestis died for love. It is strange that Norwood, who in general writes with discrimination about Euripides,[60] should so signally fail to understand Alcestis.

---

58. Haigh, *The Tragic Drama of the Greeks,* p. 300.
59. *P. W.,* VI, cols. 1246, 1267.
60. *Greek Tragedy,* pp. 323 ff.

He says that in spite of the fact that innumerable[61] readers have extolled her as one of the noblest figures in Euripides' great gallery of heroines, he personally finds her frigid, unimaginative, ungenerous, and basely narrow, in her spiritual and social outlook. In his tirade against her he makes the following statement, which is extraordinary to the point of being ludicrous. "From the beginning of her first intolerable speech we know her for that frightful figure, the thoroughly good woman, with no imagination, no humour, no insight." He adds later, for good measure, "no charm."

It is amazing that any English critic could have written this. A display of humor by Alcestis on her deathbed would be grotesque. Her first and almost her only thought is the future of her children, who may suffer if their father marries again. That most natural and inevitable thought accounts for what Norwood calls her "base and narrow social outlook."

Norwood expresses his admiration for the play as a whole with a fine appreciation that makes his attack on Alcestis as a frigid wife and humorless, antisocial woman the more amazing. We may respect her, we are told, but not love or pity her. Others[62] have understood Alcestis and her "gracious loveliness" better.[63]

Sacrificial maidens, who are slain to appease the gods, who are sometimes voluntary victims, appear in several plays. Macaria, Polyxene, Iphigenia, the daughter of Erechtheus and Praxithea, and others give the poet opportunity to express noble devotion and patriotic feeling in splendid speeches of self-sacrifice. The Athenians listened with delight to the praises of Athens and of death for her sake, which seemed all the greater tribute to the city when a woman voluntarily offered herself to die. Lycurgus,[64] the fourth-

61. *Ibid.*, pp. 189 f. 62. Murray, *Alcestis*, p. XIV.
63. J. A. K. Thomson, *Alcestis and her Hero, Greek Tradition*, p. 138. London, 1914.
Lucas, *Euripides*, p. 36. New York, 1923.
64. *Against Leocrates*, 160, 9.

century statesman and prime minister of Athens, quotes from the *Erechtheus* the long speech of Praxithea, the queen, who gives her daughter as a sacrificial victim to save the city, as she would have given her sons in war to defend Athens. He calls Euripides a fine poet and praises him for the choice of that myth for a drama, which he says "was an example to the spectators to follow, in its patriotism, its grandeur of spirit and its nobility, worthy of Athens."

In his earlier plays, Euripides often praises his native city. In the *Medea* a lovely chorus celebrates the beauty and wisdom of the city, to which "war had never come" (432 B.C. just before the outbreak of war and the invasions of Attica by the Spartans).

The *Heraclidae* and the *Suppliant Women,* the occasion of the latter of which was an outrageous refusal on the part of Thebes to allow the Athenians to take up their dead for burial after the Battle of Delium (424 B.C.) are full of patriotic fervor, and laud the humanity of Athens as the refuge for the unfortunate. The *Suppliant Women* is called in the Greek introduction to it "an encomium of Athens." Athens is contrasted with barbarous and tricky Sparta. Athens "has eyes of pity."[65] Theseus appears in the *Suppliant Women* as the ideal Athenian, as he does in the later play, the *Mad Heracles.* In the *Suppliant Women* he praises democracy, which he claims to have founded in Athens,[66] and indignantly repudiates the name of tyrant. When asked by the Theban herald where the tyrant of the country is, he says: "Athens is ruled by no one; she is free," a reminiscence of Aeschylus.[67] He also, like Aeschylus,[68] commends the "middle class that saves the state." The play suffers dramatically from its superabundance of long speeches and good sayings. One of

65. *Suppl.* 190. (Literally, "she has eyes for what is pitiable.")
66. *Suppl.* 353.
67. Aesch., *Persians,* 241 f.
68. *Suppl.* 244. Aesch., *Eum.,* 526 ff. The play also has echoes of Aeschylus' *Prometheus Bound* in *vv.* 200 ff.

these emphasizes the longing for peace that was so strong in Athens in the year in which this play appeared.

> If Death stood plain beside the voting-urn
> Our war-mad Greece would not be perishing.[69]

Theseus is a tragic and noble figure in the *Hippolytus,* losing both wife and son, the latter by his own error and because of his beloved Phaedra's lie. His passionate sorrow for his wife is the poetry of grief. There is one beautiful unforgettable line uttered by him.[70]

> Thou art gone, thou art fled, like a bird, from my hands.

In the *Heraclidae* the chivalry of Theseus appears in his son Demophon. In this play, at the end, the Chorus of Athenians endeavors to make Alcmene, the mother of Heracles, conform to the "Laws of the Greeks"[71] and refrain from killing her son's enemy Eurystheus. Alcmene's vengeful hatred prevails over the humane remonstrances of the Chorus.

This passage in the *Heraclidae* in which the Chorus of Athenians protests against the killing of the captured Eurystheus is said by Dr. A. Douglas Thompson to be the only one in Euripides where vengeance on a captured foe is deprecated.[72] Dr. Thompson quotes several passage from Euripides, the sentiment of which goes back to Solon, where the view is expressed that a man (or woman) should be bitter to a foe and loving to a friend. He does not observe that in all but one of the cases which he cites the speakers are characterized as barbarous, cruel, or maddened—Medea, Hecuba in her frenzy of grief against the treacherous murderer of her son, on whom she has just taken awful vengeance, the

---

69. *Ibid.,* 484 f. I have discussed the date of the *Suppliant Women* in *Chronology of the Extant Plays of Euripides,* see pp. 55 ff. I date it in 420, after the treaty with Argos. Aristophanes' *Peace* appeared in 421, just before the Peace of Nikias.

70. *Hippolytus,* 828.

71. See my discussion, *Chronology,* pp. 33 ff. There are references to the "Laws of the Greeks" in the *Suppliant Women,* 311, 526 ff.

72. A. D. Thompson, *Euripides and the Attic Orators,* p. 78. London, 1898.

wicked Menelaus in the *Andromache,* the poisoning peda-
gogue in the *Ion,* and Menelaus again in the *Orestes.* The
other passage quoted by Thompson is from the *Mad Heracles.*[73] In it old Amphitryo tells Heracles, who is about to
save the lives of his wife and children from the murderous
tyrant, Lycus, that it is Heracles' nature to be a friend to
friends and to hate all that is hostile, a mild form of Solon's
maxim. I do not wholly agree, however, with Paley's note on
Ion, 1045. He there says, "Euripides consistently puts this
doctrine in the mouth of a bad man." But the good old man,
Amphitryo,[74] in the *Mad Heracles* speaks of the pleasure it
is to look upon your dead enemy, in this case, the tyrant
Lycus. I agree with Nestle[75] that Euripides regarded the
avenger of evil as the instrument of divine justice. Since in
the cases adduced by A. D. Thompson the sentiment is always
in character, it is not fair to quote as the dramatist's own
opinion what one of his bad or frenzied people say. If each
character uttered only the sentiments of the dramatist, we
should have no drama. It would seem self-evident that "you
cannot credit a dramatist indiscriminately with the opinions
of his characters."[76] Euripides has suffered more than any
other tragedian in being thus misinterpreted, partly because
he is so quotable and has so many "maxims." Then, too, his
verses are often quoted out of context by those who wish to
confirm some thesis or prejudice of their own. Those who
have written in "blame of women"[77] have found a treasure-
house of abuse in Euripides. Even such a learned and finely
critical writer as Decharme[78] is entirely untrustworthy in
his use of fragments and isolated quotations to establish his
belief that Euripides hated women. He attributes wholesale

73. *H. F.,* 585 f.
74. *H. F.,* 585 f., 732 f.
75. *Op. cit.,* p. 191.
76. Lucas, *Euripides,* pp. 28 f.
77. Stobaeus, *Florilegium,* Gaisford, pp. 431–437. G. H. Macurdy, "Blame of
Women," *Vassar Quarterly,* XI (1926), 190 ff.
78. P. Decharme, *Euripides and the Spirit of his Dramas,* translated by
James Loeb, pp. 94 ff. New York, 1906.

to the poet everything that his characters may say or appear to say against women. As Lucas[79] says, enough nonsense has been written about Euripides' misogyny, and it is "merely ludicrous to bring such a charge seriously against the creator of Alcestis and Phaedra, Polyxena, Andromache and Creusa and Iphigenia." Women were one of the poet's "causes"; he was interested in their psychology, not from malice, but because he realized that they, as well as men, had minds, and were potent for good and evil.

That it was just to do good to friends and harm to enemies was a commonplace of Greek morality. Though, undoubtedly, Plato was the first Greek to prove formally the fallacy in this point of view, as he does in the famous discussion of what justice is in the first book of the *Republic*,[80] Euripides shows this fallacy by implication and example in plays in which the cruelty and folly of such vengeance are represented. The *Trojan Women* is his protest against the "rape of Melos" by the Athenians in 416 B.C., the year before the play was produced. (It got the second prize.) In other plays the deed of vengeance is so revolting that the doer of it is condemned by the Chorus, as in the *Medea,* or condemns himself, as in the *Electra.* At the end of the *Bacchae* in the scene in which Dionysus explains to Agave that he is avenging himself on her for her failure to recognize his god-head, she tells him that his vengeance is too great and that "gods should not be like mortals in their anger." In this verse Euripides, in almost the last of his dramas, as he has many times in the others, calls deity to answer before the bar of human justice, and Dionysus has no answer that meets Agave's reproach.

Euripides was a psychologist in his analysis of human emotions, a moralist seeking to make the Greek religion moral, and he was fascinated by all aspects of human life. Sophocles is called an idealist, though he is not interested in ideas.

79. Lucas, *Euripides,* p. 36.
80. *Republic,* 331 D ff.; *Crito,* 49 B f.; *Gorgias,* 469 C.

Euripides discussed "[81]the questions of the day, the double standard of morality, the emancipation of women, war, marriage, democracy, rhetoric, education." In this Weinstock sees the destruction of tragedy and of the Greek ideal. He says Euripides *"ist Ankläger, Richter und Mörder zugleich des griechischen Geistes"*—the accuser, judge, and at the same time, the murderer of the Greek spirit.

Greek tragedy had to die. It could not survive the coming of philosophic thinking. The Greek spirit was not murdered by Euripides, but transmitted by him and by Socrates to the new era which still influences the thought of the world, the era of Plato and his pupil Aristotle. The Greek spirit lived on in the philosophy, oratory, art, and theatre of the fourth century. The two men,[82] who were so often caricatured by Aristophanes in his great comedies, as seekers after new things and sophistical thinkers, inspired more than any others of whom we know the thought and art of that century. Plato without Socrates is almost inconceivable, and the humanizing spirit of Euripides appears not only in the domain of thought, in oratory, and the theatre of Menander, but also in the sculpture of Scopas and Praxiteles, their contemporaries and their successors down to the time of the Roman sarcophagi, which so often reproduce scenes from the plays of Euripides. The majestic statue of Peace with the infant Wealth in her arms by Cephisodotus might well have been inspired by the beautiful song in the *Cresphontes.*[83]

> O Peace, to all wealth-giver,
> Thou fairest of the Blest,
> I pine for Thee forever.
> Thou loveliest and best.
>
> I fear me that in sorrow
>   Old age shall come apace,
> Ere on some glad tomorrow
> I see thy glorious face.

81. Weinstock, *op. cit.,* p. 288.
82. Murray, *Aristophanes,* pp. 87 ff., 106 ff. Oxford, 1933.
83. Nauck, *Frag.* 453. My translation.

And hear the hymns outringing
Which chorused voices raise,
The dancing and the singing
    Of maidens in Thy praise.

Keep from us hate that slayeth
And faction's fires abhorred,
All maddened strife that playeth
    With the two-edged sword.

Lover of peace, lover of truth and of humanity, Euripides taught Athens, which he also loved, the gentler virtues and a higher idea of God. If in doing this he destroyed faith in the "songs of the bards" on which the older tragedy was built, the time had come when the Athenians, in their progress from their anthropomorphic religion to philosophy, should put away childish things.

"He has all Hellas for his monument." So begins the epitaph which Thucydides, his fellow thinker, or the musician Timotheus wrote after his death. Yet Athens rejected him in his old age and in the year after his death Aristophanes wrote in mockery and also in admiration[84] of him one of his greatest plays.

There is no play of his that is not infused with pity and with sorrow for the evils of the world in which he lived. He brought the problems of real life before the people whom he entertained as a dramatist, delighted as a poet, and taught as a philosopher. If he is sometimes more the philosopher than the dramatist or poet, it is all to the good. We take him as we find him and rejoice that the Enlightenment had its poet.

84. For Aristophanes' admiration and love for Euripides see Gilbert Murray, *Aristophanes*, p. 134.

XII

HUMANITY IN HERODOTUS,
THUCYDIDES, THE ATTIC ORATORS
AND MENANDER

HERODOTUS and Thucydides, men of Greek blood but of different origins, both geniuses, made an extraordinary contribution to the intellectual life of mankind when they inaugurated the study and writing of history in the fifth century B.C. We owe the word history to Herodotus. "The word had already been used by the philosophers. But while these are looking for the truth, Herodotus is looking for the evidence."[1]

The two men were contemporaries, Herodotus being the older by a term of years which is variously estimated at ten to twelve, or twenty, or even thirty years. Herodotus was born about 485 B.C. Thucydides was general in 424 B.C. To hold this office he must have reached his thirtieth year and he was probably more than thirty when elected to it. They were both friends and admirers of Pericles, who was older than either. Pericles died in 429–428 B.C., Herodotus not long after him, Thucydides in the early years of the fourth century.

Both historians show the influence of the intellectual movement which we call the Illumination or the Enlightenment (*Aufklärung*), under the Periclean democracy. Herodotus, as we have seen in a previous chapter, loved democracy and wrote with enthusiastic admiration of its early struggles and victories. Thucydides wrote in a time of disillusionment. He lived (chiefly in exile) to see the failure of Athenian statesmanship after the death of Pericles, the disasters in Sicily, and the final defeat of Athens at the end of the war. The later democracy was tarnished by demagogy and,

1. J. A. K. Thomson, *The Art of the Logos*, p. 237. London, 1935.

according to Plato, the Athenians had become "idle, chat-terers, cowardly and greedy."[2] Thucydides had seen the moral sickness that followed in the train of the plague and of the war. Writing in exile as he did, he was enabled, he says, to observe both sides.[3] His writing is not embittered by his exile, but he does not fail to note the errors of Athenian statesmanship. He intends to be strictly impartial, but in descriptions of Athens and the Athenians that occur in the speech of the Corinthian envoy[4] in his first book, and above all in the speech of Pericles in the second book of his history, there is a thrill of pride in his city, that makes us realize the glory of Athens better than if he had told us "the tale that we wish most to hear."[5]

His grim world of contemporary warfare is lighted every now and again by the splendor of his thought and his devo-tion to Periclean Athens. The orators Lysias and Andocides give us an idea of Athenian political life in the last years of the fifth century, and it is disheartening enough. The Par-thenon and the Propylaea, beautiful and unending source of pride, are there, but according to the orators man was vile. Yet, in spite of the Thirty (Tyrants), professional poli-ticians, and political and religious persecutions, the way was preparing for Plato and philosophy.

Pericles, except for his campaigning, was not often away from Athens. He had no leisure for writing. Herodotus, born in Halicarnassus on the Asiatic shore, and exiled from his birthplace, lived in Samos, in Athens, in Thurii and traveled far. He and Thucydides, both exiles from their native cities, wrote what their respective trainings, natural gifts, and

2. Plato, *Gorgias,* 515 E.
3. Thuc. V, 26.
4. Thuc. I, 70; II, 35 ff.
5. J. T. Shotwell, *The History of History,* p. 199, New York, 1939: "The greatest theme in history lay before his eyes, but it was not war; it was the Athens of Pericles and of his own time." As he wrote his history largely in exile, it is not strictly true to say that Athens lay before his eyes, and the history of his own time for him was the history of the War. A history of the intellectual movements of the time could hardly have been written then.

travels prompted them to write. Both are invaluable for what they give and both are criticized for what they fail to give and for what are called their faults. These faults have a way of turning into virtues when discussed by the more modern writers.

Herodotus was attacked in what proved to be a boomerang, by a great scholar, for mistakes and alleged mistakes about the number of toes possessed by the hippopotamus, the friendly offices performed for the crocodile by the sandpiper, and other such matters, which Sayce[6] enumerates to prove that the Father of History was the father of lies. Thucydides has his detractors who dislike the intricacies of his syntax, or his political views, his use of speeches to illustrate situations, the small content of his subject, his lack of psychology, or his omissions.

Their critics have sometimes failed to understand the habits of thought of the two first historians and their means of expression. How and Wells note that modern science has been kinder to Herodotus than Victorian criticism, and that anthropologists like Tyler and Westermarck have found most valuable evidence for the primitive history of mankind in some of the stories quoted with contempt by Mure.[7]

Herodotus from his first page sets before our eyes a motion-picture of interesting men, women, and children. In the bleak world of Thucydides women and children do not enter, except to be captured or killed. The great German scholar Wilamowitz, after speaking with a certain brutality about the famous Aspasia, says: "It is no small indication of the dignity of Attic history that only one woman appears in it, and she dominates it, the Maiden of the Acropolis."[8]

Thucydides barely mentions women in his history of the Peloponnesian War. There is the famous advice given them

6. A. W. Sayce, *Herodotus*, Books I–III, pp. XXV ff. *et pass.* London, 1883.

7. *Commentary on Herodotus*, I, 35, 36. Oxford, 1912. For criticism of the critics of Thucydides see Shotwell, *op. cit.*, pp. 212 f.

8. *Aristoteles und Athen*, II, 3, p. 100. Berlin, 1893.

in the *Funeral Oration* of Pericles, "to be talked about as little as possible, for good or evil, among men."[9] Besides the legendary Helen[10] he mentions by name the wife[11] and the daughter[12] of the tyrant Hippias and gives the epitaph which was on the tomb of the latter. He also names an Edonian woman,[13] who helped to assassinate the Edonian king, and a daughter of Perdiccas of Macedon, given by her father in marriage to Seuthes, the Odrysian king. In giving the date of the year 431 B.C. according to the various reckonings that prevailed at Argos, Sparta, and Athens, he states the name of the priestess of Hera at Argos, Chrysis, who was in the forty-eighth year of her office.[14] Her accidental burning down of the temple in 423 B.C., her flight to Phlius, and the name of her successor are told at the end of the fourth book. He mentions the insult to the sister of Harmodius, who was not allowed to be a *kanephoros* in the Panathenaic procession.[15]

These are merely formal references and no detail is given about any of these women, except the epitaph of Archedice, daughter of Hippias, and the account of the accident by which the old priestess at Argos set Hera's temple on fire.

Herodotus, in the course of his history, tells of many women, good and bad, who could easily have been heroines in a play of Euripides. A savage queen of the steppes, Tomyris is a sister to Medea in her fierceness. Herodotus tells[16] the story of her defense of her country and her revenge for her son's death. After her husband's death, according to a northern custom, she became queen, for the period of her son's minority, of her tribe the Massagetae, on the great steppe east of the Caspian Sea.

9. Thuc., II, 45, 2.
10. I, 9, 1.
11. VI, 55, 1.
12. VI, 59, 3.
13. IV, 107, 3.
14. Thuc., II, 2, 1; IV, 133, 2.
15. VI, 56, 1.
16. Hdt., I, 205 ff.

King Cyrus, after capturing Babylon,[17] and reigning there for ten years, marched to the distant northeast to subdue the tribes who dwelt there. He sent to Tomyris a proposal of marriage. "Tomyris,[18] understanding that he was wooing not her, but the kingship of the Massagetae, refused the offer." As his ruse did not succeed, Cyrus marched to the border river and made open preparations to invade the land of the Massagetae. While he was busy with the construction of his towered bridges, Tomyris sent a herald to him, asking him to desist and leave the Massagetae in peace. If that should not please him, let him give up all his trouble of bridging the river and either advance a three days' march into her territory for battle or, if he preferred, let her army cross and enter his territory.

The king took advice of Croesus, who was with him as counselor, and, acting on it, he advanced into the country of Queen Tomyris, pitched camp there, and then retired to the river, leaving in his camp tables spread with food and unmixed wine, as a lure for the unsophisticated Massagetae, who, unused to strong drink, as expected ate and drank too much and slept. The Persians, who had been left to watch for this happening, killed or captured the sleeping men, among them the son of Tomyris. The queen sent to Cyrus to demand her son, not knowing his fate. The latter, when the effect of the wine had passed off and he had realized his situation, had asked to be freed from his bonds. He then killed himself. Tomyris and her Massagetae conquered Cyrus and his army in a great battle. Cyrus was killed; Tomyris filled a goatskin with blood and, seeking out his body on the field, dipped his head in the blood, and said, reviling the dead man: "You have destroyed me, though I live and have conquered you in battle, for you have killed my son by treachery. As I warned you before, I now give you your fill of blood."

17. *C. A. H.*, IV, 10–15.
18. Hdt., I, 205 ff.

This is a story which Thucydides could not have admitted to his history. It is probably untrue in its romantic details and there is no way of testing its truth. Its dramatic and savagely human character attracted Herodotus and it makes an epic ending for the life of the great Cyrus and for the first book. There is a Greek drama in it.[19]

Herodotus says that he does not know that the story is true, but it seems to him the most probable account of the death of Cyrus.[20] Whatever kernel of truth may be in the tale of the dealings between Cyrus and the Massagetae, there are very evidently romantic additions to the facts. Herodotus would inevitably choose the most dramatic form of the tale to relate, even while expressing his doubts of its credibility.

His pages are sprinkled with the names of women, some of whose stories he tells at length, while merely mentioning the tragic deeds of others. He is aware of the part that women have often played in making history, and his sympathetic picture of Artemisia, the fighting queen of his native Halicarnassus, indicates his appreciation of women who do not conform to the ideal of his friend Pericles. He says that Artemisia furnished Xerxes with his best ships and with sounder advice than any of his other allies,[21] and tells with pride of Xerxes' remark about her gallant fighting in the battle of Salamis. "My men have shown themselves women, my women men." The king's regard for her and her speeches both before and after Salamis are told with vividness and sense of character. The proud Persian queen, Atossa,[22] who "had all the power," who desired her husband to invade

19. Cf. Shakespeare, *Henry VI*, Pt. I, II, 3.
　　　"I shall as famous be by this exploit
　　　　As Scythian Tomyris by Cyrus' death."
Also *Henry VI*, Pt. III, I, 4, where Queen Margaret gives to the Duke of York, before she stabs him, a napkin, stained with the blood of his son. Did Shakespeare read Herodotus in the translation by B. R., which appeared in 1584?
20. For other accounts see Xen., *Cyropaedia*, VIII, 7; Ctesias, *Persica*, pp. 6–8.
21. Hdt., VII, 99.
22. *Ibid.*, VII, 3.

Greece that she might have Spartan and Argive, Corinthian and Athenian women to be her handmaidens, and the apparently nonhistorical, magnificent Babylonian Queen Nitocris[23] "the great builder," were superwomen of a type that delighted Herodotus, coming as he did from a land where there were traditions of woman-rule, and he realized the value and interest of such women for his history.

No matter what subject Herodotus touches in his discursive history, whether it is the anthropology of savage tribes or theories of government, or the pride and fall of tyrants, he treats all his matter in an inquiring spirit, with humanity and with an urbane and gently ironic wit. No one else has such freshness and such an unfailing flow of interest. How and Wells[24] think he is too theological—that his work is a sermon on the text "pride goeth before a fall."[25] But he points his moral so charmingly and is often so pleasantly skeptical that one may call him the most entertaining of theologians.

The "sense of tears in human things" appears in his history in many ways, but it is in his tales about children that he most abounds in tenderness, more than any other Greek writer except Homer and Simonides. I will recount one of these stories[26] that tells of pity in the heart of a murderer, a momentary gleam of beauty in the mire of ignorance and cruelty. The story is about Labda and her son, who was destined to great things.

Amphion, one of the Bacchiads who ruled at Corinth, had a lame daughter whose name was Labda. No Bacchiad was willing to marry her, so she was taken to wife by Eetion, a man of the folk from Petra, by descent, however, a Lapith.

23. She seems to be legendary. The name is Egyptian. Cf. Sayce, *op. cit.,* p. 106 n. 4; How and Wells, *op. cit.,* pp. 185 f. She is, perhaps, Nebuchadnezzar, masquerading as a woman. Cf. J. B. Bury, *Ancient Greek Historians,* p. 71. New York, 1909.

24. *Op. cit.,* I, 43.

25. Cf. J. A. K. Thomson, *Art of the Logos,* pp. 121 ff., 145 ff.

26. *Hdt.,* V, 92.

Because of various oracles which said that Labda's son would be a rock to crush, or a lion to devour those who ruled at Corinth, and that he would be a judge over Corinth, the Bacchiads, on learning that a son was born to Labda sent ten of their number to Petra to kill him. When the ten men reached the house, they entered the courtyard and asked to see the baby. Labda, knowing nothing of their purpose, and thinking that they wished to see the child because of their good will to his father, brought the baby and laid him in the arms of one of them. They had been planning as they came along the road that the first one to receive it should dash the child to the ground. So then, when Labda brought the child and the first man took it, the child by some divine chance smiled at him, and when he perceived this, pity kept him from killing it. He passed the child to his neighbor and he to his, and so it went, passed on through the whole line of ten men, and no one of them had the heart to kill it. They gave it back to its mother and went out, and, standing at the door, blamed one another bitterly, especially the man who had first taken the child, because he had not acted according to their agreement. Finally they decided to go into the house again and all together murder the child. Labda had been listening to them behind the door, and hid the child in a place where they would not be likely to look for him, the meal chest. They made their search, but did not find the baby. So they went back and told those who had sent them that they had fulfilled their orders. The baby grew up to be the great Cypselus, named from the chest, *kupsele*, in which he had been hidden.

"In the Story of Cypselus," Professor J. A. K. Thomson says,[27] "see how the interest is focussed on the child, although its own powers of expression are limited to a smile." Only one other child[28] in Greek literature, the baby Astyanax in

27. *The Art of the Logos*, p. 187.
28. But I must not omit the baby Perseus, in the *Lament of Danae* (Simonides).

his nurse's arms, cowering back in them in fear of Hector's great plumed helmet, can rival this laughing infant.

This story of Labda and Cypselus appears to me to be easily first among all stories for its picture of human nature and simple tenderness. It is, as Professor Thomson says, "a sort of narrated drama"; he quotes from the *Treatise on the Sublime* (where the author is commenting on a passage in Herodotus): "Do you see how he takes over your soul and leads it—making hearing sight?"

The story of the *Childhood of Cyrus,* the casting away among desolate hills of a babe adorned with gold ornaments and richly clad, discovered and taken to his hut by a cowherd, is a version dramatically and vividly told of an ancient tale of which there are many forms. The tears of the cowherd's wife over the plight of the beautiful little boy, her successful plan to save his life, and the pity of these humble folk contrasted with the cruelty of the king are related simply and naturally, with no striving after pathos. Professor Thomson[29] has translated this tale or *logos,* with a discussion of the antiquity of its type, which is familiar to us from the famous story of Oedipus.

The *Art of the Logos,* from which I have quoted, is an invaluable study of the Traditional Story. I know of no other book that so convincingly reproduces the essential quality of Herodotus and reveals the secret of his style. I will borrow one more passage from the book before going on to discuss the feeling for humanity and the gentler virtues in that despiser of *Logoi,* Thucydides.[30]

"Herodotus, while at all times obeying or commanding the genius of the Logos, is of course more than a simple Logopoios. He is a great man revealing, especially in that part of his book where he is less bound by the tradition, an ardent but candid patriotism and an enthusiasm for beautiful and noble things."[31]

29. *Op. cit.,* pp. 152 ff.   30. Thuc., I, 22, 4.
31. *Op. cit.,* p. 142

If I have done him less than justice in omitting so much that testifies to the civilized and humane mind of this "perhaps the most typical Greek all round that ever lived,"[32] it is because the *Art of the Logos* has set all this forth so fully and so adequately.

The absence of gods,[33] women, and children from the work of Thucydides has often been noted. He desires to write only what is relevant to his subject, the Peloponnesian War, the importance of which he perceived at its inception, and at once began to write its history.[34] There is, however, one episode[35] which is totally without influence on the course or result of the war, which he allows himself to relate because of its atrocity. It is the massacre of school children, just assembled for their lessons, at the hands of bloodthirsty Thracians, who were running amok. There is no political significance in the incident, only mad cruelty. J. B. Bury's theory that Thucydides is not interested in questions of good or evil, but only in political expediency will not work in this case.[36]

These Thracians had been hired by Athens in 413 B.C. to sail with Demosthenes to Sicily in his expedition to reinforce Nikias and his men. Arriving from Thrace too late to sail, they were put in charge of Diitrephes, an Athenian general, to be conducted back to Thrace, as they were too expensive for Athens to maintain as auxiliary troops. Diitrephes sailed with them up the Euripus, touching here and there, as he had been told in Athens to use the mercenaries to attack enemy towns, if a chance offered. He gave the Thracians a free hand, and, after a raid on Tanagra, led them to Mycalessus, a little old town some miles up from the coast which, never dreaming of any attack from the sea, had let its walls crumble and left its gates open. The Thra-

32. *Ibid.*, p. 143.
33. Cf. R. W. Macan, *C. A. H.*, V, 405, 406.
34. Thuc., I, 1. Cf. 21, 22.
35. *Ibid.*, VII, 27, 29.
36. Bury, *Ancient Greek Historians*, pp. 138 ff.

cians rushed into the town and killed every living thing in sight, having no mercy on young or old or on brute beasts. They fell upon a boys' school where the boys had just entered and massacred them all. Thucydides, who had Thracian blood in his veins and lived a large part of his life in Thrace, says: "The Thracians, when their spirits are high, are the most blood-thirsty of barbarians." He is always sparing in comments on the events which he relates, letting his facts speak for themselves. Here, however, after telling of the butchery of the boys, he adds that in all the horror in Mycalessus, with every form of destruction to be seen on every hand, this was the most horrible of all the atrocities.

At the end of the fifth book he tells of another work of destruction. In the famous long dialogue between representatives of Athens and of the island of Melos, which had had a long history of civilization, the Melians were asked to surrender their independence and join Athens against Sparta, though they were of Dorian blood. The Athenians argued that they had the power to make Melos surrender. The Melians refused, relying on the rights of their case. The Athenians besieged the island, found traitors to help them, and the Melians were forced to put themselves at the mercy of Athens. The Athenians killed all the adult men, sold the women and children into slavery, and colonized the island with five hundred settlers of their own.

A damning statement, which still has power to stir the blood against the tyrant city Athens and her realistic politics. And we are asked by J. B. Bury[37] to believe that in the *Dialogue,* that "horrible conversation"[38] as Cornford calls it, in which Athens sets forth her shameless standpoint that he who has the power has the right, and in his passionless brief statement of the destruction of Melos, Thucydides had no intention of holding the conduct of Athens up to obloquy. He is, according to Bury's theory, merely interested in the

37. Bury, *op. cit.,* pp. 139 f.
38. *Thucydides Mythistoricus,* p. 179.

political situation and eliminates all "conventional sentiment and morality."[39]

I think that few readers of the *Melian Dialogue* agree with Bury. Cornford is undoubtedly right in saying that the only significance of the *Dialogue* is the moral significance, and that Athens was mad and blinded with the thirst for gain. "So the historian saw her; so also did Euripides."[40] And it was not only intellectuals and extraordinary men like Thucydides and Euripides who felt the shame of Melos; it lingered in the memory of the man in the street, who knew of it and had seen the *Trojan Women* enact on the stage such horrors as his city had so often caused. And when, eleven years later, the news of the lost sea fight came to Athens and was relayed by moaning voices from the Peiraeus to the town, the Athenians knew that they too were to be besieged by Lysander's ships, as Melos had been by theirs.

And that night no one slept, but they mourned for their dead and much more for themselves, thinking that they were now to suffer such things as they had done to the Melians, who were colonists of Sparta, when they overcame them by siege, and to the Histiaeans, and the people of Scione, of Torone, of Aigina, and to many others of the Greeks.[41]

So Athens after the Battle of Aegospotami feared that her treatment of Histiaea, Scione, Torone, and Aegina would now come home to her and that she would be repaid for her atrocities in her own coin. The extermination of the people of Scione is told by Thucydides[42] in practically the same words as those used of the treatment of Melos. "About the same time in this summer [i.e., of 421 B.C.] the Athenians took Scione by blockade, killed the men of adult age, enslaved the women and children and gave the land to the

39. *Op. cit.*, p. 144.
40. Cornford, *Thucydides Mythistoricus*, p. 187. Cf. the whole chapter, *The Melian Dialogue*, pp. 174 ff. A. E. Zimmern, *The Greek Commonwealth*, p. 437; W. S. Ferguson, *C. A. H.*, V, 281; Finley, *op. cit.*, pp. 55 ff.
41. Xenophon, *Hellenica*, II, 2.
42. Thuc. V, 32.

Plataeans." Cleon had proposed this measure and it had been carried in the Assembly two years before, after the revolt of Scione in 423 B.C. Cleon,[43] the successor of Pericles in political power, "the most violent of the citizens, who at that time [427 B.C.] had the greatest influence over them,"[44] had made a similar proposition to kill the men and enslave the women and children of Mitylene, which had seceded from Athens. The Assembly voted in favor of the proposal, the words of which evidently were destined to become a sinister formula for the punishment of cities that objected to Athenian rule. A trireme was dispatched with orders to their general to destroy the people of Mitylene at once. On the next day a change of heart came to the Athenians and a realization that they had passed a resolution of extraordinary cruelty in dooming the whole city to destruction rather than the guilty only. Thucydides gives two speeches, one in defense of Cleon's measure and one attacking it. Cleon in his speech angrily reproached the Athenians as a futile and changeable democracy, unfit to rule an empire, and looking for a better and more ideal world than the world of reality in which they lived, as though they were listening to the lectures of sophists, instead of deciding about the good of the city. He urged his hearers to forget mercy and moderation, the "greatest foes of empire," and punish ruthlessly.

The speech of Diodotus which opposed Cleon's measure, on the ground that terrorism was no advantage to Athens, argued that the death penalty did not decrease offenses, or deter criminals, and in this case would only alienate sentiment from Athens. He expressly disavowed "mercy and moderation" as motives for his plea, quoting the words from Cleon, and he stressed the expediency of lenient action.

Bury holds that this speech gives Thucydides' own point of view; namely, that only expediency and not mercy should weigh in state matters. The rôle of justice "was slight and

43. *Ibid.,* IV, 21, 3; III, 36, "demagogue and rabble-rouser."
44. *Ibid.,* III, 36.

subordinate" in him; "the dramatist could not ignore it, though he allows it as small a range as he can; the thinker dismissed it."[45]

If, as Bury thinks, Thucydides was *not* interested in the fact that his city massacred entire populations, and if he was concerned only to consider whether such action was expedient for the city, it is interesting to find Diodotus (his spokesman) here arguing that such merciless treatment of peoples is *never* expedient for the one who punishes. Diodotus is pretending to leave mercy and decency out of account and beats Cleon with his own weapon of expediency. That the fate of Mitylene meant much to Thucydides is seen in the tense and vivid narrative[46] that follows the speeches.

After various speeches pro and con, the Athenians were divided in opinion; the vote was very close, but the motion of Diodotus prevailed. Another trireme was at once dispatched, in the hope that it might catch up with the first one, which had a day and a night's start, in time to save the city. The envoys from Mitylene provided wine and barley for the sailors and promised them great rewards if they should arrive in time. The sailors were so eager that they ate the barley kneaded with oil and wine while rowing, and they slept and rowed by turns. By good luck no wind blew against them and the ship ahead was sailing with no speed, since their errand was a detestable one. As the first ship sailed so slowly, the second one reached the harbor just after her. Paches had already read the decree and was about to execute it when the second ship came in and prevented the massacre. So close did Mitylene come to destruction.

Thucydides shows an interest in the fate of the city whose men Cleon would have had massacred as the men of Scione were massacred six years later. He applies the word repugnant to the errand of the first trireme and speaks of the measure advocated by Cleon as extraordinarily savage.

45. Bury, *op. cit.*, pp. 142 f. Cf. Finley, *op. cit.*, pp. 47 ff., for parallels between these speeches and passages in the plays of Euripides.
46. III, 49.

These bloody resolutions to destroy whole Greek communities[47] must have been profoundly shocking to the finer spirits in Athens. It would be hard to believe with Bury[48] that Thucydides regarded them with indifference and was interested solely in "the logic of policy." In writing, as it is agreed[49] that he wrote the Melian episode, years after the event—years of disaster for the Athenian policy—Thucydides surely set down with intent those last arrogant words which in the *Dialogue* the Athenians uttered as a final taunt to the doomed Melians. There is no greater example of pride soon to be brought low and replaced by bitter humiliation, suffering, and death. I quote Cornford's beautiful translation of the famous lines of Aeschylus about the pride of Xerxes, which apply as well to proud and cruel Athens.

> The flower of pride hath bloomed, the ripened fruit
> Of suffering all is garnered up in tears;
> You who have seen the reapers' wages told
> Remember Athens.

In his third book, writing about the moral degradation and the corruption caused by the war of parties in Corcyra, Thucydides writes thus about peace and war.[50]

"In times of peace and prosperity both states and individuals have higher ideals, since they are not driven against their will by irresistible forces. War destroys the means of daily life and is a cruel master, working on the passions of the multitude and forming them in the image of the state of war."

So the ex-soldier and student of the campaigns and politics of the Peloponnesian War writes about the effects of war.

---

47. The city of the Melians had been founded seven hundred years before the Athenians destroyed it. The island had been a centre of culture in the Minoan Age.

48. *Op. cit.*, pp. 140 ff.

49. *Op. cit.*, pp. 80 f., 264; Classen, *Thukydides*, I, XXXVI ff.

G. B. Grundy, *Thucydides and the History of His Age*, pp. 501 ff. London, 1911.

50. Thuc., III, 82, 2.

In general he gives the detailed account of the campaigns without comment. When he does speak of moral issues, as in the terrible account of the loss of all decencies in Corcyra because of the civil strife, or in his comments on the heroism and the moral weakness manifested during the attack of the plague in Athens, his high standards of honor and decency appear.

"No one has ever smiled over a line of Thucydides," says a great scholar[51] and historian. He never strives for pathos, but no one can read unmoved his account of the sufferings of the Athenian army in Sicily after the naval battle.[52] He brings out with deep feeling the irony of the contrast between the exultant hopes with which they had sailed, "intending to enslave others," and the horror of their present state. Thucydides has told here as no one else had ever told of men "who did what men will do and suffered all that men can bear."[53]

These were his own countrymen, men of the Athenian Empire, which had not long to last. Cornford has rightly seen and shown that for Thucydides these things were not only "the accurate facts, so far as they could be ascertained,"[54] but tragedy. He had no belief in gods to help or hinder him in his stern "search for truth."[55] The more tender emotions which women[56] and children bring into life were banished from his history, but he shows by his terrible picture of the savagery of the Corcyraeans,[57] and their total loss of all the civic virtues, his hatred for war and all its works and his love for the mercy and moderation which the demagogue Cleon denounced.

51. Macan, *C. A. H.* V, p. 418.
52. Thuc. VII, 70–75.
53. *Ibid.,* VII 77. Cf. Cornford, *op. cit.,* p. 220.
54. Thuc. I, 22.
55. *Ibid.,* I, 20.
56. The only active service of women mentioned by him (V, 82, 6) is their participation in the building of the Long Walls, reaching to the sea, which the Argives raised against the Spartans in 418 B.C.
57. Thuc., III, 81 ff.

The only love of which he speaks is the love of Athens.[58]
This he preserved during all the corruption which increased
under the demagogic leaders in the long years of the war.
He was one of her greatest sons, and in exile from her wrote
his work that so nobly keeps Athens in the memory of the
civilized world.

Grundy[59] remarks that good and evil as understood by
Thucydides are good and evil as understood by the best
among mankind today. Ancient Greek parallels to the standards of right and wrong by which the average man of a
civilized community today measures conduct are to be found
in the so-called Attic orators, professional writers of speeches
for others as well as political speakers in the Assembly, who
give us real information, all the more valuable because they
reveal themselves and their clients more or less uncon-
sciously. We get the best pictures of Athenian life and character at the end of the fifth and early part of the fourth centuries from Lysias. As Earp says, "he has a unique power of
sinking himself in his subject."[60] He writes with extraordinary versatility for various sorts of clients, ranging from the
rich young aristocrat who is accused of having served in the
cavalry in the time of the Thirty to the disreputable crippled
old "ward-politician," who shared the exile and return of
the democratic party and wishes to keep his little pension.
The young aristocrat is a candidate for the Senate and is
undergoing a scrutiny of his life. He describes himself as
having no bad habits or companions. He neither drinks nor
gambles, nor does he associate with cheap and idle young
men. In public and private life he manifests the democratic
virtue of moderation *(metriotes)* and its companion virtue,
reasonableness *(epieikeia* = Matthew Arnold's "sweet reasonableness"). The two words, *metrios* and *epieikes,* as I have
noted before, are used, often with *kosmios* and *sophron*

58. *Ibid.,* II, 43.
59. Grundy, *op. cit.,* p. 9.
60. F. R. Earp, *The Way of the Greeks,* pp. 11 ff. Oxford, 1929.

(orderly and controlled), by the democratic writers of the fourth century to describe a good citizen, sometimes with the addition of *philanthropos,* philanthropic.[61] Mantitheus, the young aristocrat who delivers the speech, admits that he is ambitious and perhaps overready to speak in the Assembly. He had fought for Athens in the Battle of Corinth.[62]

He has been generous, he says, to his two sisters, settling them in marriage with good dowries, and also to his brother. He does wear his hair a little long, which was regarded with suspicion at Athens, as indicating aristocratic and Spartan sympathies, but on the whole he is a young man after the heart of the Athenian public—"we are the only sort you think worth a penny." This speech is Lysias at his best, in his gift of natural and brilliant rendering of character. The date of the speech is about 392 B.C. and we see in it the importance attached in the early fourth century to the civic virtues.

In Lysias' other speeches for all sorts of characters he writes in the same bright and easy manner, marked by naturalness and simplicity. He expresses in all of his speeches, written for public or for private occasions, the devotion to Athens and the emphasis on the civic virtues that are in evidence in the speech for Mantitheus. Of the Golden Rule and of forgiveness of an enemy Lysias has no more conception than any of the other orators. In his first speech, the only one written for himself, *Against Eratosthenes,* he says that while he would consider it to be a crime against religion, if he should ever take the name of the defendant on his lips if it would help him, he is willing for the sake of doing him harm to speak to the man himself, thinking that to be a holy and religious act. The man had helped bring about his brother's death. No other view than that of the rightness

61. Cf. Carl Becker, *Yale Review,* XXVIII (1939): "When Democratic Virtues Disintegrate," p. 660, "the democratic virtues—of reason and sound judgment, of good will, of tolerance and humane dealing."

62. A marble monument of a young knight of his company, Dexileos, remains in Athens.

of retaliation, which is doubtless the view of the vast majority of men today, is found in any of the orators. Isocrates[63] expresses the feelings of the natural man when he says: "When the two courses are open, neither of them commendable, it is better to choose to do atrocious things to others rather than have them done to one's self." "Any one who has sense," he says, "would so choose, but perhaps a few of those who lay claim to wisdom would deny it."

Plato said that it was better to suffer wrong than to do it.[64] This belief of Socrates and Plato finds no echo in the orators.

It is inevitable that women and children should have a much smaller part in the speeches, private and public, than men. Lysias speaks of them simply and naturally, sketching the Attic housewife in her good and her bad aspects. There[65] is the young wife whose husband trusted her completely, only to find himself deceived by her and her lover with the help of a dishonest maid. The narrative is extraordinary for the picture which it gives of an Athenian bourgeois interior. It is told with such verisimilitude that it hardly differs from stories that are told today in modern courtrooms or in the newspapers.[66] The young wife so thrifty, at first the best wife in the world, looking so carefully after the baby and the household, the husband devoted to his wife and child, a little strict with her but always kind, the seducer, a roué, who caught sight of the young wife when she went to her mother-in-law's funeral, and bribed her maidservant to arrange a rendezvous, the trickery of the wife lying to her husband, while her lover was in her chamber, the old woman sent by a former mistress of the lover to inform the husband of his wife's intrigue, the discovery of the guilty pair in bed

63. *Panath.*, 117.
64. *Crito*, 49 B; *Gorgias*, 469 B, 508 D–E; *Republic*, 335 B ff., 336 A. 336 A.
65. *Lysias*, I.
66. Ph. E. Legrand in *The New Greek Comedy*, translated by James Loeb, p. 521, New York, 1917, mentions this speech first in a list of Attic orations which have many qualities in common with the New Comedy.

by the husband who came in with torches and friends; how the husband bound the seducer's hands, accused him, then struck him down—all this is told with a power of word painting in simple direct language that is something new in Attic prose. Only Herodotus can tell a story with such vividness. Euphiletus, the husband, was protected by the Attic law, which permitted the penalty of death to be exacted by the injured party not only for adultery, the seduction of a wife, but also in the case of concubines "who are less worthy."[67]

In another speech[68] an Athenian lady, a widow, whose father has taken advantage of his guardianship of her children to embezzle their fortune, makes a moving appeal to him in the presence of friends and witnesses. She is not accustomed to speak before men, but her misfortunes compel her to plead her children's cause. She calls her father to account for the money which he has wrongfully kept and then addresses him in such moving words that none of those listening could speak for emotion and none went away dry-eyed.

She said:

You have had the heart to deny that you kept all their money, which their father deposited with you, and that which I put in your hands at his death. And you have seen fit to turn your grandchildren out of house and home, with nothing but the shirts on their backs, barefoot, with no attendant, with no bed to lie on, no garments to put on, without the household goods their father left them, without the funds which their father deposited with you. And you bring up my step-mother's children in luxury and wealth, and that is as it should be, but you wrong my children, whom you have driven with insults from their home and are striving to make beggars when they have been rich. For such actions you have no fear of the gods, nor shame before me who know all that you have done; you have no regard for your brother's memory, but you value money above us all.

67. *Ibid.*, 30.
68. *Lys.*, XXXII.

This speech is said by ancient writers to be among Lysias' best works. It shows as fully as any of them and with more emotion than most how excellent he is at representing real people with a convincing simplicity and plainness. His characters have a life that is hardly to be found in any other of the ten orators of the so-called Canon.[69] Since we get from him more than from the others an idea of the ordinary morality prevailing in private life in Athens, it has seemed worth-while to dwell on his work rather than on that of the others, from whom we learn much about Athenian laws and politics, but get a much dimmer and less varied picture of Athenian men and women. Before Lysias the actual Athenians about whom we learn are chiefly statesmen. In him the everyday citizen makes his appearance as an individual. That citizen at his best is a lover of democracy, a good husband and father, a good friend, orderly, self-controlled and honest, proud of Athens and ready to fight her battles. Among his bad citizens are men whose faults and vices are the opposites of the virtues just mentioned. He wrote on sophistic subjects[70] before he became a professional speech writer, but he does not bring his philosophy into his eminently practical speeches. He has the Periclean attitude toward women, and in one[71] of his speeches speaks of ladies who lived so discreetly that they were ashamed to be seen even by their male relatives. He speaks with admiration of mother love, saying that it is the nature of a mother to endure ill-treatment from her children and to be grateful for what they do for her, however small it is.[72] Duty toward parents was one of the strongest of Athenian compulsions and next to it came regard for wife and children. These feelings are so frequently expressed in Lysias and the other orators that there is hardly need for illustration.[73] Love of

69. Jebb, *The Attic Orators*, pp. 63 ff. London, 1893.
70. Plato, *Phaedrus*, 227.   71. III, 6.
72. *Lysias*, XXXI, 22.
73. Lycurgus, *Against Leocrates*, 94 ff.; *Lysias*, XIII, 91; *Androcides* I, 74, etc.

Athens and patriotism appear in the fourth-century orations, sometimes expressed sincerely and nobly, by Lycurgus and Demosthenes, sometimes as "the last refuge of a scoundrel," perhaps by Aeschines,[74] and certainly by the author of pseudo-Demosthenes LIX. Antiphon,[75] who was killed in 411 B.C. as an oligarch and member of the government of the Four Hundred, is highly praised by Thucydides, who says that he made the greatest defense ever made, in the memory of his time, by a man on trial for his life. Lysias and Andocides and Isocrates believed in democracy. About Isaeus, who was a writer of speeches and a specialist in the law of property, Dionysius in his discussion of him says that he does not know whether he had any politics at all.[76] The younger orators, Demosthenes, Aeschines, Lycurgus, Hyperides, and Dinarchus, belonged to the period of the political and military struggle with Macedon. Aeschines, though belonging to the Macedonian party in politics, is ostensibly patriotic.

The most important speeches of the fourth century are the great political orations of Demosthenes. These are full of a burning patriotism and love of Athens, and bitter hatred of her enemies, whether Macedonians or Athenian traitors who worked for Macedon. The story of his struggle is famous. "His very faults all sprang from the excess of his loyalty and devotion to his country. He failed, but the gods gave him one of their highest gifts, to fail greatly in a great cause."[77]

The private speeches of Demosthenes often contain bitter attacks on individuals, written with all his tremendous power of invective. In one celebrated case[78] his own low standard of professional ethics is revealed by the fact that

74. Jebb, *op. cit.*, p. 397.
75. Thuc. VIII, 68.
76. Dionysius, *Isaeus,* 1.
77. W. W. Tarn, *C. A. H.*, VI, 460.
78. Dem., XXXVI. *For Phormio,* about 350 B.C., XLV. *Against Stephanus,* 350–349 B.C.

he wrote, within the space of a year,[79] speeches for a defendant and for a prosecutor in the same case. It is a stain on the
record of Demosthenes that he paid Apollodorus for his political services in moving to transfer the Theoric Fund to the
war budget by writing for him a speech of incredible violence, attacking the very man for whom he had written his
fine speech *"For Phormio."* This was a reproach in his lifetime[80] and still testifies against him. If every politician has
his price, the price stipulated by Demosthenes for selling
his private honor was that the buyer should do something to
help preserve the freedom of his beloved Athens.

To propose to divert the Theatre Money[81] to any other
purpose was a serious legal offense with heavy penalties attached. Apollodorus in 348 B.C. was convicted of proposing
illegalities and heavily fined. The prosecutor was Stephanus,
acting for Eubulus, the finance-minister and leader of the
Peace party.[82] Eight years afterward Apollodorus appears in
the speech *Against Neaera,* written and chiefly delivered by
himself, but introduced by a man who was his son-in-law
and also his brother-in-law. This speech, important histori-
cally because it gives an account of the attempt of 348 B.C.
to divert the Theatre Money, is also important for the light
which it throws on marriage and concubinage in Athens,
and on the position of the class of women called *hetaerae,*
who were usually not Athenian by birth. The speech makes
a celebrated distinction between wives, hetaerae, and pal-
lakai (concubines).[83]

The speech is one of the basest of the extant Attic orations.
I will discuss it briefly, since it betrays the heartlessness and
callousness of the unscrupulous politicians who were active
in Athens in this period[84] of stress and dread of war, and

79. Cf. Sandys and Paley, *Select Private Orations,* XXVII, XXXVIII,
XXXIX ff.; F. Blass, *Attische Beredsamkeit,* III, 1, 413 ff. Leipzig, 1877. Drerup,
Aus einer alten Advokatenrepublik, p. 50. Paderhorn, 1916.

80. Aeschines, II, 165; Plut. *Dem.,* XV.

81. P. Cloché, *Démosthènes,* pp. 18 f., 86 ff. Paris, 1937.

82. *Ibid.*   83. [Dem.] LIX, 122.

84. About 340 B.C.

because of its kinship with the New Comedy. It reveals the low morality of *l'homme sensuel moyen* in Athens, which appears in the unblushing statements of Apollodorus, who is in the same breath hypocritical censor of morals and shameless expositor of sensuality. The speech, as Legrand[85] has seen, is intimately connected in spirit with the New Comedy, although the speaker Apollodorus displays nothing of the sense of chivalry and sympathy that appears in Menander.[86] The writer in his *aperçus* of character and episode and his power of telling a story is a loquacious and coarsened Lysias.

The law was very severe on the non-Athenian who was convicted of marrying a native Athenian. The penalty was to be sold as a slave and in the case of a foreign man there was added the confiscation of his property. There were many evasions of this law, which itself contributed to the growth of the class of *hetaerae,* such as Aspasia, cultivated and intelligent "foreign" women of Greek blood, who were unable to marry Athenians because of the law, which had been enacted by Pericles[87] himself before his connection with Aspasia. Foreign-born men, even if they had been slaves and were non-Greek, often became Athenian citizens.[88] This speech shows with what ease children not legally eligible could be entered on the lists of the demesmen.[89] Apollodorus himself was the son of a wealthy banker who had been a foreign-born, non-Greek slave, and his mother was also an ex-slave. We have very unflattering descriptions of Apollodorus in the two speeches by Demosthenes which I have mentioned. In the first one, written in defense of the stepfather, Phormio, Apollodorus is said to be a habitual black-

85. Legrand, *op. cit.,* p. 521.
86. Murray, *Aristophanes,* pp. 227 ff.
87. Plut., *Pericles,* XXXVII.
88. Their wives appear to have become *astai,* citizens also. Cf. Archippe, wife of the banker Pasion. They were the parents of Apollodorus.
89. Cf. the charge of Aeschines (III, 99, 159) that Demosthenes with a "half Scythian" mother had been illegally enrolled in his deme.

mailer,[90] dishonest, and noted for consorting with courtesans. Even in the speech written by Demosthenes for Apollodorus the latter describes himself[91] as an ill-bred man, not up to the Athenian standard for a gentleman, with an ugly face, a bawling voice, and a rowdy gait. Evidently his unpleasant personality was so unmistakable that it seemed the more strategic policy for Demosthenes to have him admit it freely.

In the speech *Against Neaera,* Apollodorus, Neaera, her daughter Phano, and the other persons who appear in the course of it resemble the low types of the New Comedy, which "dealt with the present, not the past."[92] In particular, the procuress Nikarete, a married woman with a good Attic name, singularly inappropriate to her profession (it means Virtue Victorious), a Greek "Mrs. Warren," with an eye for beautiful and clever little girls whom she trained to be *hetaerae* on a grand scale, calling them her daughters and chaperoning them about Greece with their lovers, is at once a living person and a character for Menander's stage. Neaera had been living for thirty years as his wife with the politician Stephanus, who had acknowledged her children as his. She is prosecuted in this speech by Apollodorus, on the ground that she was not Athenian-born and therefore not legally married to Stephanus. At the time of this trial she was over fifty years old and a grandmother. Her daughter Phano had been twice married to Athenians and twice driven out when they discovered that she was not the daughter of an Athenian mother. Her first husband, whose conduct Apollodorus commends, cast her out when she was with child and refused to give back her dowry. Then he fell ill and had no one to take care of him, since he had quarreled with all his kin. His wife and her mother came and nursed him—"You know what it means to have a woman to nurse you and look after you when you are sick," Apollodorus re-

90. Dem., XXXVI, 45, 54, 55.
91. *Id.,* XLV, 77.
92. Murray, *op. cit.,* p. 238.

marks—and the man, softened by their kindness, decided to recognize the child as his son. As soon as he recovered his health, however, he married an Athenian woman, and kept the dowry of Phano. This conduct is applauded by the speaker.

The speech dwells chiefly on the career of Neaera as a *hetaera,* although, as Blass[93] remarks, the character of Neaera's life had nothing to do with the charge plainly stated at the end of the speech—"this charge which I have brought against Neaera that she is a non-Athenian married to an Athenian." Apollodorus, without a drop of Greek blood in his veins, the son of two foreign-born slaves, was not really shocked at the marriage of a Greek woman from Corinth or Megara to an Athenian. In the speech against Stephanus (not the husband of Neaera) that Demosthenes wrote for Apollodorus, he says that his stepfather Phormio, the banker, was a barbarian,[94] unable to speak Greek correctly. This must also have been true of his own ex-slave parents, Pasion and Archippe.

It is an evidence of his political influence that he calls as witnesses against Neaera the two most distinguished men in Athens—old political enemies, but now (340 B.C.) drawing together to face the war threat from Macedon—Eubulus,[95] the famous finance-minister of Athens and member of the Peace party, and Demosthenes. Eubulus testified that when he was a young man, he used to visit Stephanus and Neaera when she was living as a *hetaera* and that she drank in company with them. Stephanus, who married Neaera, was at that time a political follower and friend of Eubulus. Demosthenes testified that he had been present when Stephanus was challenged by Apollodorus to hand over four maid-servants belonging to Neaera, to be examined by torture, a challenge which was refused. The torture was to elicit a

---

93. Blass, *op. cit.,* III, 1, 539.
94. Dem., XLV, 30.
95. Cloché, *op. cit.,* pp. 18 f.

statement that Neaera's children were not children of Stephanus.

Theomnestus, who starts the speech, says that he prosecutes Neaera in order to revenge himself on Stephanus, who prosecuted his relative eight years before. Stephanus at that time acted for Eubulus, as Apollodorus acted for Demosthenes. Now that the two principals had drawn together[96] in view of the coming struggle, Stephanus might prove an obstacle to the new plan for applying the Theoric Fund to the defense budget. This was done in 339 B.C. on motion of Demosthenes.

Neaera and her daughter Phano were caught up in the whirlwind of politics and their petty lives were threatened with ruin because of the action of Stephanus of eight years before. If Apollodorus tells the truth about Neaera in the stories which he repeats from dissolute old men, who had known her in her prime, she had been an accomplished and beautiful *hetaera,* who was taken by her lovers on journeys to every part of Greece and overseas to Chios. She had the art of pleasing her lovers, who desired to see her well placed, when they decided to settle down and marry. They later all contributed money to help her to buy her freedom. At this point (in 371 B.C.) Stephanus met her in Megara and married her. Several of Apollodorus' witnesses testified that she drank at the symposia, a mark of a *hetaera.*[97] Two of the beautiful naked *hetaerae* on the psykter by Euphronius in the Hermitage have drinking cups in their hands and one is drinking while a third is fluting. Many a Neaera bathing, dancing, or drinking may be found on black-figured and red-figured vases.

The result of the prosecution of Neaera is not known. It is likely that Stephanus, who had been a man of influence

---

96. Drerup, *op. cit.,* pp. 120 ff., 127.

97. Cf. *Isaeus,* III, 14, for the propriety of conduct required of an Athenian married woman. "They do not go with men to dinners, nor eat with men outside the family."

in politics[98] and, as this prosecution shows, was a power still
to be reckoned with, may have succeeded in extricating himself from this difficulty as he had from so many in the past.
Since it was common knowledge that Neaera had lived with
him as his wife for thirty years, it is probable that he would
be allowed to keep on living with her in free union.[99]
Apollodorus nowhere actually proves that she was not
Athenian-born. If she was, she would be the legal wife of
Stephanus. Compare the similar case of Chrysis in the "Sa-
mian Woman," by Menander.

The fate of the seven beautiful little girls who were
bought by Nikarete, and are said by Apollodorus to have
been given their freedom by lovers who bought them from
the procuress, is typical of the times in which they lived.
"The women and children sold into slavery," of whom we
so often read in Thucydides, were of good Greek blood and
filled the slave markets of the Greek and foreign world. It
is no wonder that the New Comedy tells so constantly of
the panders, procuresses, and the ruined girls of good family,
who are their stock in trade.[100] It is remarkable that Apollodorus should know all the names of Nikarete's girls, Antaea,
Stratola, Aristocleia, Metaneira, Phila, Isthmias, and Neaera.
He tells of the orator Lysias taking Nikarete, Metaneira, and
Neaera to be initiated, Neaera being a little girl. This would
be before 380 in any case, as Lysias died in or before that
year. Apollodorus' habit of going back over forty years for
his accusations throws suspicion on all his highly colored
tales. Demosthenes speaks of his notorious association with
hetaerae and also says that what Apollodorus says is not
evidence, but lying talk.[101]

This speech of Apollodorus, so near the New Comedy in
spirit, was delivered in 340 B.C. when Menander, the chief
poet of that Comedy, was two years old. As Legrand has seen,

98. Aeschines, II, 140; IG, II, 109, 5; Dittenberger, Syll.,³ 205.
99. Cf. Murray, op. cit., p. 228.
100. See Murray, op. cit., pp. 229 ff.; Legrand, op. cit., 92 ff.
101. Dem., XXXVI, 60.

the New Attic Comedy is descended not from Euripides only, but also from the dramatic speeches of the Attic oratory, from such speeches as that of Lysias in behalf of the murderer of Eratosthenes and this speech against Neaera. The speeches, vivid and realistic, are usually partisan, scurrilous, and bitter, aiming only at gaining a favorable verdict; the comedy of Menander was "a comedy with thought and with tears in it."[102] "The last of the Attic writers,[103] Menander, who carried on in his comedies the tradition of Euripides, has had an enormous influence on the stage. His work remains in scanty and fragmentary form and is also known to us by plays of the Roman comedy by Plautus and Terence. Tarn[104] finds him and his school "the dreariest desert in all literature." Gilbert Murray[105] perceives "Menander's philosophic spirit, his interest in women, his inexhaustible human sympathies and profound tenderness of heart." He has been attacked from early times[106] for the monotonous and repetitious characters of his plots. To quote Tarn[107] again, "Life is not entirely composed of seductions and unwanted children, coincidences and recognitions of long lost daughters, irate fathers and impertinent slaves." But the wit, wisdom, and humanity which Menander puts into the development of his plot and his portrayal of character make the meagreness of invention in the plots immaterial in comparison with the spirit of his drama.[108] Many of us can endure any amount of repetition of both plot and character in the novels of Mr. P. G. Wodehouse,[109] who has

102. Murray, *op. cit.*, p. 240.
103. M. Croiset, *Revue des Deux Mondes*, L (1909), 806 ff.
104. Tarn, *Hellenistic Civilisation*, p. 280. London, 1930.
105. Murray, *Aristophanes*, p. 261.
106. Cf. Legrand, *op. cit.*, pp. 237 ff.
107. *Op. cit.*, p. 240.
108. "Il a peint ses contemporains tels qu'il les voyait et il les a bien vus." Croiset, *op. cit.*, p. 831.
109. Miss J. R. Bacon in a paper entitled *Plautus and Posterity* has compared the Jeeves cycle in Wodehouse to the plots of Plautus. Cf. *Proceedings of the Classical Association*, XXXIII (1936), 38.

said in reply to the criticism that his story is always about the same people that it is, moreover, always the same story about the same people. Legrand points out that the Greeks have never attached importance to originality in their art, and that their tragedy, narrative poetry, sculpture, and architecture are open to the charge of monotony, as well as the New Comedy.[110]

Menander has the same love for the gentler virtues as has his intellectual ancestor, Euripides. The field in which he worked, the depiction of contemporary life, gave his wit and irony a greater scope than was afforded in the plays of the tragedian. He has no magnificent outbursts of patriotism and hatred for the enemies of Athens, to match those in Euripides and Demosthenes. The times were changed. Demosthenes was dead, Athens defeated, and politics taboo on the stage. Hector's words, "There is but one good omen, to defend our fatherland," so natural in a warring world, had lost meaning for Athens under the heavy hand of Macedon. "The gaiety mingled with seriousness"[111] of the New Comedy gave Athens intellectual life and pleasure in her time of political humiliation, and handed on the tradition of the theatre to many languages as yet unformed. And Menander wrote one famous verse, the spirit of which has not yet been realized, in spite of Christian teachings. It is as familiar as are quotations from the Bible and Shakespeare and known even to the ignorant in its Latin form. Menander wrote it in his play *Heauton Timoroumenos,* which Terence translated.

Homo sum, humani nil a me alienum puto.[112]

Even Euripides, to whom Menander is so akin, has nothing so universal in its spirit as that. "The audience," says

110. *Op. cit.,* pp. 514, 515.
111. Plutarch, *Quaest. Sympos.,* VII, 8, 3, 7.
112. Terence, *Heaut.* I, 1, 25. "I am a man and think that all that touches man is my concern."

St. Augustine,[113] "though composed of stupid and unculti-
vated people, applauded this verse."

A remarkable fragment remains in Menander's own polished[114] and suave Greek. I quote it in Gilbert Murray's
translation.

> I count it happiness
> Ere we go quickly thither whence we came,
> To gaze ungrieving on these majesties,
> The world-wide sun, the stars, water and clouds,
> And fire. Live, Parmeno, a hundred years
> Or a few months, these you will always see,
> And never, never, any greater things.
> Think of this life-time as a festival
> Or visit to a strange city, full of noise,
> Buying and selling, thieving, dicing stalls
> And joy-parks. If you leave it early, friend,
> Why, think you have gone to find a better inn;
> You have paid your fare and leave no enemies.

113. cui sententiae ferunt etiam theatra tota plena stultisque indoctisque
applausisse. *Ep.*, CLV, 14, Migne; *Patrologia Latina* (Paris, 1902), XXXIII,
col. 672. Cf. Plutarch, *Moralia*, p. 854 B.

"Why is it really worth while for an educated man to go to the theatre
except to see a play of Menander's?"

114. Plutarch, *op. cit.*, pp. 853 D, E.

XIII

THE GOLDEN RULE IN
SOCRATES AND IN CHRIST

IN THE development of Greek art each form starts
from crude, almost unconscious beginnings and finally
reaches the perfection of beauty appropriate to its kind.
In the field of ethics the simple tribal morality, achieved
before the period of the epic and finding expression in it,
developed, as the Greek spirit expanded, enlarged by the
thought and form of epic, lyric, philosophy, drama, and
history, until it came to its perfection in Socrates and Plato
with their vision of Eternal Beauty and Eternal Goodness.[1]

I have referred to the civic virtues which are mentioned
so often in the orators, who give us a picture of everyday
life in democratic Athens. They are wisdom, for which there
are three words—*phronesis*, intelligence, *episteme*, understanding, *sophia*, knowledge; *dikaiosyne*, justice, which often
comprehends *eusebeia*, piety; *sophrosyne*, temperance, moderation; and *andreia*, courage. Of course there were many
other names for good qualities besides these cardinal virtues,[2]
but this "Pythagorean tetrad" appears often in Plato. In
the early dialogues which have the name of a virtue for an
alternative title, Socrates attempts to discover the essential
nature of each virtue. In the *Crito* the true meaning of
justice is sought. Temperance is discussed in the *Charmides,*
in the *Laches* courage, and in the *Protagoras* the relation of
all these three to knowledge, of which Socrates proves the
others to be parts.[3]

This famous Socratic identification of all virtue with

1. Plato, *Symposium,* 210, 211. Cf. 211 D. "Man must live contemplating
Beauty."
2. Cf. C. Ritter, *Platon,* II, 507 n. 1. Munich, 1910.
3. *Protagoras,* 327 C, 349 f., 361.

knowledge is also reported by the unphilosophic Xenophon in the *Memorabilia*.[4] He says:

He did not separate knowledge and temperance, but held that the man who knew and followed beauty and goodness, and knowing what was base avoided it, was both wise and temperate. He said that justice and all the rest of virtue was knowledge. For both just acts and all acts that are done by virtue are beautiful and good. Those who know these things (justice and virtue) cannot choose anything in their stead and those who do not know them cannot do these things, and if they try, they fail. Since just acts and all that are beautiful and good are done by virtue, evidently justice and the rest of virtue is knowledge.

Plato, looking at the virtues that make the character of the good citizen and the good state, sees them *sub specie aeternitatis,* as partaking of the Idea of Good, "which supplies objects of knowledge with the truth that is in them and gives to him who knows the power of knowing them." "This Idea of Good[5] is the origin of knowledge and of truth, and while both are beautiful, both knowledge and truth, you will rightly consider that this is other than they, and still more beautiful." The objects of knowledge derive from the Idea of Good their real existence and their power of being known, just as the sun affords to visible objects the power of being seen and also their power of generation, growth, and nurture, though it is not itself the power of generation.

To what extent Socrates, who was interested in practical ethics of conduct, inspired or shared in the Platonic doctrine of the eternal ideas or forms cannot be known. We have the testimony of both Xenophon and Plato that he was the "best, wisest, and most upright of men."[6] It seems probable that his greatest pupil, Plato, understood his mind and

4. Xen., *Mem.*, III, 9, 4 ff.
5. *Republic,* 508 E.
6. Plato, *Phaedo,* 118.
   Xen., *Mem.* IV, 8, 11. It has been suggested that Xenophon had read the *Phaedo.*

thought as the simpler-minded soldier and country gentleman could not, even though he, like Plato, knew Socrates
personally. As Constantin Ritter says,

In any case, Plato, of all the pupils of Socrates, has understood
him best; and in addition to that fine understanding for others
which we recognize with admiration in all his character-sketches,
he possessed the greatest gift for depiction. So his Socrates, even if
transfigured by the poet in Plato, is certainly the true Socrates, not
merely truer than the Socrates of Comedy, but also than the
Socrates of Xenophon, though Xenophon offers some valuable
additional evidence.[7]

"Platonism is love of the unseen and eternal cherished
by one who rejoices in the seen and temporal."[8] This
definition of Platonism suits the teacher Socrates as well as
his pupil, the philosopher. Burnet says, "The soul of the
man who stood transfixed in silent, brooding thought for
twenty-four hours in the camp at Potidaea is surely the soul
to which we must look for a psychological explanation of
the beatific vision described in the Phaedrus. On what else
can his thought have been concentrated during that day
and night? Surely not on the things he discusses in the
Memorabilia." The Socrates of that work could not have
inspired Plato.

In Plato's greatest dialogue, the Republic, Socrates, seeking with his friends to find "justice, a thing more precious
than many pieces of gold,"[9] arrives at a statement[10] which
is the equivalent of the Golden Rule, uttered by Christ.[11]
The principle is reached in Plato after a reasoned argument.
In the New Testament it is a command of Christ, given to
his disciples. In the Republic, as a result of the discussion,
Socrates states that a just man will not injure any man who-

7. Ritter, op. cit., I, 71.
8. J. A. Stewart, "Platonism in English Poetry," in English Literature in the
Classics, p. 30. Oxford, 1912.
9. Republic, 336 E.
10. Ibid., 335 B.
11. Matthew, VII, 12.

soever, not even the wicked and his enemies. "For if anyone says that it is just to repay to every man his due and understands by this that harm is owed by the just man to his enemy and help to his friends, he who says this is not wise, for our argument has shown that it is nowhere just to injure any man."

What Socrates here sets forth, assailing the time-honored Greek rule that it is right to help a friend and injure a foe, is familiar to everyone in the words of Christ,[12] "Ye have heard that it hath been said, Thou shalt love thy neighbor and hate thine enemy; but I say unto you, Love your enemies and pray for them that persecute you."

"Therefore all things that you would have men do to you, do you even so to them."

Xenophon[13] reports that Socrates accepts the ordinary rule of retaliation against an enemy. In the course of a conversation with Critobulus about friendship, Socrates remarks, "You have recognized that it is a man's virtue to surpass his friends in doing them good and his enemies in doing them harm." It is far more probable that Plato gave the true representation of the morality of Socrates. But the important thing is that we have in the *Republic* and also in the *Gorgias* the thought expressed that mercy is better than "justice," or rather *is* justice in the true conception of that term. This thought had not been uttered definitely before Plato, though the tragedians implicitly make it clear that it is "better to be wronged than to do wrong." Antigone's fate is felt to be better than that of Creon, and sympathy in tragedy is always with the victim of cruelty.

In the *Gorgias* the result of the long discussion is given by Socrates as follows. "In all that we had said, while the others are disproved, one statement stands firm, namely that a man must take more care to avoid doing injustice than suffering it, . . . that, next to being just, it is good

12. Matthew, V. 44 ff. Cf. Luke VI. 27 f.
13. *Mem.*, II, 6, 35.

to be made just by undergoing punishment." "Allow a man to call you a fool and insult you, if he will; yes, by Zeus, let him strike you on the cheek;[14] you will suffer no harm if you are really a good man and live in the practice of virtue." "Let us take for our guide what our argument indicates to us as the best way of life, to live and die in the practice of justice and every other virtue."

The resemblance of the thought expressed here and elsewhere in the *Gorgias* to the teaching of Christ is clear. It seems probable that Nietzsche had the *Gorgias*[15] and its teaching in mind when he attacks "Socratism," as well as Christianity, as examples of "slave-morality," and "the degenerating influence, that with subterranean vindictiveness, turns against life." "Christianity is Platonism for the folk,"[16] in contrast to the *"Herrenmoral,"* which is advocated by Nietzsche, and also by Callicles in the *Gorgias.* Nietzsche complains[17] that the gentler virtues, "pity, the helping hand, the warm heart, humility," attain to honor in "slave-morality," Socratic and Christian, and says that the "morality of pity, which seized and infected even the philosophers is the most sinister symptom of our European culture."[18]

Since Nietzsche was a Greek scholar and familiar with the *Dialogues* of Plato (he calls his own philosophy "inverted Platonism"),[19] it is interesting to find that Callicles in the *Gorgias,* who denounces the unmanly virtues of the many,[20] which, he says, result from their own impotence, and advocates the "strong man," who tramples underfoot the codes and laws that are against nature, anticipates Nietzsche's "great man," who is a law to himself, who is *"au fond* a

14. *Gorgias,* 486 C; *ibid.,* 508 D.
15. Cf. the argument in *Gorgias,* 469, *et pass.*
16. *Jenseits von Gut und Böse, Vorrede.*
17. *Ibid.,* 260.
18. *Genealogie der Moral, Vorrede,* 5.
19. E. Bertram, "Umgedrehter Platonismus," *Nietzsche,* p. 315. Berlin, 1922.
20. *Gorgias,* 492.

magnificent blonde beast,"[21] and must have "a *quantum* of brutality in him and a leaning toward crime." Callicles' "great man" is the prototype of Nietzsche's "superman" in his contempt for law and in his "natural right" to have more than the weaker.[22] Nietzsche's antagonism to Socrates, to Platonism in most of its aspects, and to Christianity, and his coupling[23] of Christianity with the teaching of Socrates indicate in many well-known passages of his works how close he felt Socrates, with whom he says[24] "he wages unceasing war," was to Christ in his preaching of the gentler virtues. In his famous early work, *"Geburt der Tragödie,"* he attacks both Euripides, "the poet of aesthetic Socratism," and Socrates himself as anti-Dionysiac and typical decadents, and he continues the attack on Socrates and on Christianity until the year of his mental breakdown. He speaks with contempt of the Golden Rule[25] as formalizing the herd instinct. Though he has been called much more the "Anti-Sokratiker"[26] than the "Anti-Christ," he sometimes speaks of Socrates and Plato with some appreciation of their greatness.[27]

I have cited well-known passages from Nietzsche because he was a Greek scholar and at the same time the most violent antagonist of all that Socrates represents; also because in reading the *Gorgias* his writings are recalled to mind constantly by the speeches of the *advocatus diaboli* Callicles, as well as by those of the young sophist Polus.

Plato in the *Gorgias* puts before us Socrates in perhaps his most brilliant demonstration of the folly of cruelty and retaliation. The dialogue contains some of his noblest utterances. He will not admit that the "strong men" of

---

21. *Genealogie der Moral*, 11; *Wille zur Macht*, 951, 968, *et pass.*
22. *Gorgias*, 483 D.
23. Cf. *Das Problem des Sokrates*, Götzen-Dämmerung, pp. 244 ff.
24. Bertram, *op. cit.*, pp. 308 ff.
25. *Wille zur Macht*, 925.
26. K. Joël, *Nietzsche und die Romantik*, p. 291. Leipzig, 1905.
27. *Der Wanderer und Sein Schatten*, 86.

this world, Archelaus of Macedon, or the Great King of Persia, are "happy" (i.e. fortunate, blest by the gods) until he knows what their condition is in the matters of training and justice. We know that "training and justice" in the mouth of Socrates means moral excellence, or, as he calls it,[28] "the good of the soul." He was put to death, as Callicles, in the *Gorgias,* prophesies that he will be. That victory for his opponents was a triumph for Socrates and his teaching, giving him immortal fame as "the best, wisest, and most just man the world had yet seen." These are the last words of the *Phaedo.*[29]

There is no nobler document in the history of morality than his *Defense.* He defines his business in life thus:

I have no other business but to go about persuading you all both young and old, to care less for your bodies and your wealth than for the perfection of your souls, and telling you that goodness does not come from wealth, but it is goodness that makes wealth or anything else, in public or in private life, a good thing for men. If, by saying this, I am perverting the young, so much the worse; but if it is asserted that I say anything else, that is not true. Therefore, Athenians, you may listen to Anytus or not; you may acquit me or not; for I shall not change my ways though I were to die a thousand deaths.[30]

The "justice" of the Platonic Socrates comprehended all the higher morality of the Greeks from the *aidos* of the Heroic Age, the Unwritten Laws which Antigone obeyed, the *sophrosyne* of the early Athenian democracy, and the humanity and pity of Euripides, who said,

> He is a boor who sheds no tear in pity,
> And base who helps not others in their need.[31]

The vision of the Platonic Socrates of absolute justice, absolute beauty, absolute goodness, which are perceived

28. *Apology,* 29 D, *et pass.*
    Gorgias, 486 D, 527 D.
29. *Phaedo,* 118.
30. Translated by Cornford, *Greek Religious Thought,* p. 187, New York, 1923; *C. A. H.,* VI, pp. 304 f.
31. Euripides, *Frag.* 407.

in their true reality by the intellect alone, is like the vision of another great teacher who wrote in Greek, much of whose doctrine has, like that of Socrates, become part of the higher moral thinking of the civilized world. St. Paul is truly Platonic when he says: "For now we see in a glass darkly, but then face to face; now I know in part, but than shall I know even as also I am known."[32]

"The earliest spokesman of the young Hellenic race felt deeply the pity of things and adjudged pitifulness to be the highest human and divine attribute."[33] The epic *aidos*, regard for others, especially the helpless, and *themis* established right, both conceptions arising from and corresponding to the needs of the society of the Heroic and the Iron Age, were expanded and chiefly replaced by the conception of *dike* which grew into *dikaiosyne*, the abstract justice. Hesiod's *dike* is sometimes the "wild justice"[34] of revenge, and the goddess Dike is joined with the spirits of vengeance, the pitiless Erinyes.[35] But Hesiod's nobler aspect of justice, itself enlarged in the *dikaiosyne* of Euripides—"nor evening-star nor morning-star more beautiful than this"[36]—came to include all the virtues that the necessities and the higher nature of the Greeks discovered. In Plato's *Republic* the definition of justice[37] according to Simonides, which is "to pay to each man what is owed him, namely, good to friends and ill to foes," is changed in the course of the argument to the statement that it is never just to injure any man. Plato's "anticipation of the Christian ethical theory"[38] is

32. Cf. *Phaedo*, 67 A f. "And when we are thus purified and released from the folly of the flesh, we shall, in all likelihood, be with others in the same condition, and know of ourselves whatever is pure; and that is surely truth." Cornford's translation.

33. Farnell, *Higher Aspects of Greek Religion*, p. 108. New York, 1912.

34. Bacon.

35. Aeschylus, *Ag.*, 1482 f., *Eum.*, 511 f.; Sophocles, *Ajax*, 1390, *Trach.*, 808 f.

36. Aristotle, *Ethics*, 1129b.

37. *Republic*, 331 E.

38. Adam, *Republic of Plato*, I, 21 n. Cambridge, 1926. Cf. *Republic*, II, 379 E.

close to St. Paul's injunction[39]—"Owe no man anything, save
to love one another, for he who loves his fellow-man has fulfilled Law." The love and pity in the epic for those of one's
own family and tribe, which is transcended even in Homer,
find their perfect and universal expression in the words of
the four great teachers of the beauty and worth to mankind
of the gentler virtues, Euripides, Socrates in Plato, St. Paul,
and Christ. Love, *agape,* is the fulfilment of law, *nomos,* and
of *aidos,* mercy, and of *dikaiosyne,* justice.

"If there be any other commandment, it is summed up in
this word, Thou shalt love thy neighbor as thyself. Love
worketh no ill to his neighbor; love therefore is the fulfilment of law."

39. Romans, XIII, 8, 10.

INDEX